HEADS YOU WIN, TAILS YOU WIN

ALSO BY RAY DIRKS

The Great Wall Street Scandal

WITH LEONARD GROSS

HEADS YOU WIN, TAILS YOU WIN

THE DIRKS INVESTMENT FORMULA

Ray Dirks

STEIN AND DAY/*Publishers*/New York

First published in 1979
Copyright © 1979 by Raymond L. Dirks
All rights reserved
Designed by David Miller
Printed in the United States of America
Stein and Day/*Publishers*/Scarborough House
Briarcliff Manor, N.Y. 10510

Library of Congress Cataloging in Publication Data

Dirks, Raymond L
   Heads you win, tails you win.

   1. Speculation.   2. Investments.   I. Title.
HG6041.D55   332.6'45   78-27174
ISBN 0-8128-2581-0

To My Clients

Acknowledgments

To Nicholas Murat Williams for his research assistance, to Lillian Danovaro and her staff for their secretarial help, and to all my colleagues and friends whose knowledge has added to my own, my grateful thanks.

Contents

HEADS YOU WIN, TAILS YOU WIN

CHAPTER 1
Heads You Win, Tails You Win

How would you have liked to watch the great stock market slide of October-November 1978, in the serene conviction that your own investments were solid? To have anticipated, in those weeks of panic selling, the profits you would soon be making by purchasing securities reduced to a fraction of their worth? To be involved in an investment program that can double your money every three to five years? To see many of your investment dollars be worth ten times as much in only nine years?

Consider the above as commitments. By the time you've finished this book, you'll know how to take the guesswork—and the nightmares—out of investing in common stocks. You'll know a great deal more about investing than the average retail stockbroker. You'll be equipped to turn your dreams for capital growth into realities. But before I make good on those commitments, let me vent a little steam.

I'm a Wall Street insider. I make millions of dollars trading in securities, for my firm, my clients, and myself. I am building the fastest-growing research operation in the business. But the reputation I cherish most is that of a maverick. I go after giant companies when I feel they're deceiving the public. I've been called the Ralph Nader of Wall Street, an identity I wear proudly. I believe in people and distrust institutions. And I am sick and tired of seeing the little man get the hell kicked out of him by Wall Street's institutions every time he buys securities.

The great selling spree of the fall of 1978 cost the small investor far more than it did the big institutions. The little man panicked and sold at a loss. The professional stood by, waiting to pick up his securities at a fraction of their value for a turnaround profit. It happens every time.

I believe fervently in the free enterprise system, but I don't see much future for it if the average investor gets mauled over and over again. For the nation's industrial machinery to function it must have capital—and it's the average investor who still supplies the bulk of that capital. It's only natural for him to squirrel his money away rather than get his nose bloodied again.

It's time this nonsense was stopped. It's time we took the mystery and fear out of investing for the average investor. It's time he—*you*—realized that there is, by God, a way to invest in common stocks without getting hurt, that there *are* excellent, even fabulous profits to be made, that investing in American companies *is* the most sensible way for Americans to build their equities in a period of unremitting inflation.

The kind of investing I'm talking about is, in all likelihood, unlike anything you've done before. When you've bought common stocks in the past, you've undoubtedly done so because your broker recommended that you do. But there was no connection between you and the company of which you were suddenly a part owner, no intimacy to the transaction, no feeling on your part that you really knew what you were doing.

I'm going to argue that buying securities at the suggestion of your stockbroker is, with rare exceptions, the worst thing you can do.

I'm going to propose a method that will make you an

infinitely better advocate of your financial interests than your broker—or any broker, myself included.

I'm going to suggest a connection in which you *do* know what you're doing, one that has human voices at the other end, people who will tell you what you need to know in order to act rationally and intelligently in your own interest. Suddenly, you'll be ahead of the crowd, in a position to make the kind of money that has always been made by Wall Street's insiders. The kind of money I've made for years.

Please take note of my terminology. Not once have I used, or will I use, the term "investing in the stock market." If I have my way about it, you'll never again make another decision in terms of the market once you've read this book. You'll never lose another night's sleep over whether the market is going up or down. The investing method I'm going to teach you doesn't require an "up" market to make you money. If you're investing correctly, you can make money regardless of what the market does. In fact, a depressed market can provide you with opportunities for the greatest profits of all. *Heads You Win, Tails You Win* means exactly what it says: Barring a total collapse of the American economic system—in which case everything you have will be worthless—there is no way you can lose in the long run if you follow the rules.

The Trouble With Alternative Investments

The most suspect man in the world is—or ought to be—the one who promises to make you money. No one can guarantee that you won't lose money when you invest, regardless of the investment. A depression can bankrupt your bank. You can invest in a choice piece of farmland, only to see a drought turn it to dust. Fire can destroy your home, and your insurance might not cover the cost of rebuilding. I can no more guarantee that you'll make a profit if you invest in common stocks than I can guarantee your safety if you leave your home to go to work.

But you will leave home today to go to work, or shop or amuse yourself, first because you have to and second because you want to. It's the same with investing. You both have to and want to make your money appreciate.

For the last several years, inflation in the United States has averaged 7 percent a year. If you had put $10,000 under your mattress on January of any given year, at the end of the year it would have been worth approximately $9,300 in terms of what the money could have bought a year before. After two years the original $10,000 would have been worth $8,650. At the end of five years, $6,960. Obviously, that's no solution.

A savings account isn't that much better than hiding your money at home. Suppose you're earning 5 percent on $10,000. The interest is $500 a year. But there's tax to pay on the interest. Assuming you're in the 40 percent bracket, the tax would be $200, making your net return $300. But there's still inflation, whittling away at the value of your money at the rate of 7 percent, or more, a year. So by year's end, the real value of your original $10,000 is $9,600, or less, even though you've invested the money. After five years, you're down to approximately $8,000. No solution there either.

Insurance? *Never* as an investment. You should have a life insurance policy, but it should be the cheapest life insurance you can buy. If you own anything other than term insurance, the chances are you've been gulled. If you're 50 now and you bought a $100,000 whole-life policy 25 years ago, you've paid premiums of $1,250 a year, or a total of $31,250 in cash. The cash value of your policy would be $35,000. Superficially, this sounds terrific: You've been insured and you've still got your money. In fact, it's terrible. Your original dollars are worth far less than they were when you paid them, and you've received almost nothing for the use of your money during all this time.

Good quality corporate bonds yield 9 percent, sometimes as much as 10 percent. But that's 4.5 to 5 percent after taxes, assuming you're in a 50 percent tax bracket. Even if you're in a 30 percent bracket, the tax on your profit reduces your earnings to a point below the rate of inflation.

A second deed of trust yielding 12 percent a year gives the person in a 40 percent tax bracket an after-tax profit of 7 percent—which puts him no better off than dead even.

Real estate: It's been a marvelous investment since the end of World War II, as every homeowner knows. Owning a home—assuming it's in accord with the kind of life you want to lead—has been and probably will continue to be an excellent cornerstone of any family investment program.

But the kind of money we're talking about now is beyond that you've used for establishing your home plus a reserve for emergencies. Should that money be in real estate? If you're sure you won't need the money at once and if you can find an attractive investment, real estate may well be a fine choice. But those are two very big ifs.

Real estate isn't fluid. You can't get your money on short notice. To get the price you want—the price that makes the investment worthwhile—may require a wait of months or years. If you simply have to have the money, then you could be forced to sell at a price so low that your profits would disappear.

It gets down to this: You have to invest your money if you want it to retain its purchasing power, to appreciate in value, or both.

To get the kind of return that will merely keep you even requires a more adventurous investment than a savings account.

Real estate, gold, and other precious objects, antiques and

paintings are fine investments if you know what you're doing, but when based on others' subjective impressions of value, they can be dangerously speculative. They are also highly illiquid. Once you own something, you have to find a buyer.

Given all these considerations, the case for investing in common stocks would appear to be overwhelming.

They can be bought and sold in an instant.

While they are vulnerable to emotion and subjective impressions, their real value in the long run is established by arithmetic.

They can more than offset the erosion of the dollar, *if* you pick them correctly.

A New Investing Concept

The traditional response to the average common-stock investor has been to let someone else do the picking for him. For a variety of reasons, that simply doesn't work.

Mutual funds offer diversification, but over the years most of them have done no better than average—meaning not well at all.

Investment counselors aren't a realistic alternative, either. First, they're expensive. Second, their services aren't widely available to those with less than $100,000 to invest. Third, and most important, even investment counselors are susceptible to fads—and by following Wall Street's prevailing fads during recent years they have managed to lose a lot of people a lot of money.

To be perfectly blunt about it, most mutual funds, institutional investors, and retail brokers have been doing a rotten job.

I'm positive you can do better.

As I said, I can't guarantee that you'll make a profit if you invest in common stocks. What I *can* do, however, is teach you a simple formula that will take as much of the risk out of investing as can possibly be taken.

What I *can* do is show you a method more conservative by far than investing in blue chip securities—and, paradoxically, with a far better prospect for impressive profits.

What I *can* do is show you how I make money by investing in securities, how I intend to invest in the future, and what I expect to achieve.

What I *can* do is show you how to take the mystery out of when to buy and when to sell, using a formula so simple that all it requires is a knowledge of elementary arithmetic.

What I *can* do, in short, is show you a whole new concept of investing—one that, unless the law of averages is suddenly repealed, virtually guarantees that you'll make an excellent return.

I'm not suggesting that you won't have to work. You will. You can't make the kind of money I'm talking about just by calling your broker. But it's not difficult work. There is nothing arcane or esoteric about it; one exposure and you've got it. It's no more complicated than buying a house. It's helpful to be able to read a balance sheet, and you'll know how to do that before we're finished, but even that isn't necessary.

The only tools you'll need for this work are available free in your public library. But you can do the work, if you prefer, without ever leaving home. You'll just have to put out a little money for subscriptions to one or two financial publications.

If you feel insecure about making the effort yourself, make your investigation a joint project with your mate. Or form an investment club with a few friends, dividing the tasks and reporting back to one another. As a further safeguard, you might want to review your findings with your accountant. Believe me, he'll be grateful to be let in on what you've found.

Once you've learned the system, you'll know how to find a splendid investment before its discovery by Wall Street pushes up its price. You'll profit at Wall Street's expense, instead of vice versa. That's exactly how I function.

I didn't always function that way, and when I didn't I lost money.

The Experience That Changed My Life

The last five years have been terrible ones for most investors. The stock market has gone nowhere, relative to where it was when the period began. In the interim, however, the market has been vulnerable to such giant swings that many small investors have been picked clean. Even many of the big institutions have done terribly, their clients losing millions of dollars with each market downturn.

I have a different story to tell. The last five years have been the most profitable I've ever had.

My change in fortune dates from 1973. Before that year I had made a lot of money in the market—and I had lost a lot of money. Since then I have made a lot of money, period. Of the 200 stocks in which I've taken positions either for myself, my firm, or my clients, 85 percent have been sold at a profit or could be sold at a profit as of this writing. With a few exceptions, the remaining 15 percent have been sold for a modest loss. All but three of the stocks that sold at a loss could have been sold at a profit had they been held, but they were sold so that the money could be invested in stocks that would appreciate at a faster rate.

During this period—a period in which the stock market wound up in a range 15 percent lower than the one in which it began—the value of my investments increased 400 percent. A few of my clients lost money: investors who bought stocks, then sold them and closed their accounts the moment the stocks went down. But of the clients who have been with me for more than a year, not one of them has lost money. Of all my clients, my favorite on the basis of performance has to be a Midwesterner who began investing with me in 1970. He has held some 20 stocks in that time. What is more impressive than the fact that his money has tripled is that not one of those stocks was a loser.

Nineteen seventy-three was the year in which I unwittingly became one of the best-known stockbrokers on Wall Street. I exposed what is generally conceded to be the largest fraud in the history of finance—involving the Equity Funding Corporation of America. The story of that fraud and my part in uncovering it has been told at length elsewhere, particularly in my own book, *The Great Wall Street Scandal.* The story I want to tell here is what happened to my investment practices as a consequence of that experience. What happened was, in a word, everything.

I'm a gambler by nature. There was a period in my life when I would bet on two dozen basketball games a week. My gambling streak was reflected in my business decisions. Prior to the Equity Funding scandal, I did a lot of speculating. I tried to make countless short-term gains. Often I succeeded, but sooner or later I would have a loser—the kind of loser that can wipe out all your gains. On one occasion, I went broke. I learned that you can make money fast for awhile, but not forever.

My pattern was a familiar one. I've known many successful investors who would make 200, 300, even 500 percent gains on their investments—then put all their money in one stock that went down 100 percent. Men who had so much money that they couldn't spend it all if they devoted all of their time to spending. Men who because of a single speculation wound up right back where they had begun.

The Equity Funding scandal gave me the scare of my life. Here was a glamorous, burgeoning corporation that had become a darling of Wall Street. Large institutions had bought hundreds of thousands of its shares, which at one point had risen to $80 a share from an original price of $3, on the basis of impressive annual increases in earnings. The only trouble was that the earnings were bogus: Equity Funding had no profits. The company was inventing business, "selling" insurance policies to persons who never existed, then reselling these policies to other insurance companies.

The experience drove home to me, as nothing else could, how fraught with risk investing can be. Who really knows what's going on? When a company can manage to hoodwink the Securities and Exchange Commission, the New York Stock Exchange, hundreds of stockbrokers, its own auditors, many of its own employees, most of its directors, and three state regulatory bodies, what chance has the average investor?

That was the question that haunted me in the wake of the Equity Funding scandal. It drove me to a complete rethinking of the way in which I invested money for my clients and myself. It led me to the set of principles that are the subject of this book.

I know who's made money investing in securities and I know who hasn't, and those who have have generally followed the principles set forth in this book. I've made mistakes investing, and the mistakes, I see now, were made when I didn't follow those principles.

Luckily, I had never invested in the securities of Equity Funding. Had he adhered to the principles I now follow, no prudent investor would have bought the stock, either.

Not for a moment do I believe that American corporations make a practice of the kind of hanky-panky that Equity Funding practiced. To the contrary, the one cheerful consequence of that lamentable episode was that it made investing a lot safer than it had previously been. Today, we can be much more certain that the facts and figures by which corporate life is measured are exactly as stated. Corporate officials are much more conscious of the need to disclose information properly. Stock exchange officials are much more willing to suspend trading in a stock if there is any question at all as to whether a corporation has failed to make public everything it should. In 1973, a halt in the trading of a stock was a rarity; between 1974 and September 1978, there were 2,662 such halts.

Five years ago, only an insider could get the information needed to make big money in securities. Today that information is available to everyone.

In the last chapters of this book, I'm going to show you why I believe that in the last 100 years, there hasn't been as good a time as now to invest in securities; why great values can be bought for such astonishingly low prices; why you can expect to see your money increase at the rate of 20, 30, even 40 percent a year, with only a minimum of risk.

In the meanwhile, what I hope to persuade you to believe is that if you want to make this kind of money, you've got to invest for yourself. The one promise I can make without reservation is that I can teach you how.

CHAPTER 2
The Case Against Your Broker

I'm not going to win any Wall Street popularity contests for saying this, but it's my view that the average stockbroker is not the man you should listen to when you invest your money.

First of all, your interests and his interests are inherently contradictory. Most of the time it's in your interest to hold securities for a long time. He earns a commission only when you buy and sell securities. Holding a stock requires patience, and that's one thing stockbrokers generally don't have; when they advise you to hold a stock they're taking money out of their own pockets. That's tough for anyone to do. Even if your broker were a saint, he would be under a certain amount of pressure from his firm to generate commissions.

Second, there is the matter of a broker's qualifications. There are striking exceptions, of course, but the average broker is not a trained investment counselor. He is a salesman. He may have been a very good salesman before he became a broker, but little if anything in his experience would have prepared him to be an expert in the securities business. He would have a peripheral knowledge of the business from his daily activity plus his reading of reports and newspapers, and he might even have an extra measure of common sense. But by and large he would not have to know a great deal to do what he does. The test required for becoming a stockbroker has gotten much tougher in recent years, but the average high school graduate who is willing to take a course for a few weeks can pass it.

And yet, this is the man to whom so many investors give discretion in the investing of their money, in the belief that he knows what he's talking about. One indication of how unwise even the large brokerage houses consider this arrangement is that they have been discouraging discretionary accounts in recent years on the grounds that the average broker isn't qualified to manage a client's portfolio on his own.

What the average broker does become good at is passing along to you information developed by his firm. He represents his firm as having strong research capabilities, analytical prowess, and the kinds of contacts that can develop inside information. The arguments he uses to convince you to buy and sell securities are almost all supplied to him by the brokerage firm he works for. But the sense he conveys to you is that he is an equal partner in this information-gathering process.

In fact, the average retail broker is the least well-informed person in his firm. In the pecking order of the securities business, he is the last to know.

The dangers of this for you are enormous. It is highly likely that everyone else in the firm has already acted on the information before it gets to your broker. Let's consider the consequences of that.

Suppose your broker gets a report from his firm's research division to the effect that the XYZ Corporation looks as if it will have a great year and that its stock ought to be bought at the current price. By the time your broker gets that report, The firm's largest investors will have already acted on it. They feel that they're entitled to get information before anyone else gets it, and, to keep their business, the firm obliges them. As a consequence of all this activity the price of the stock will have risen anywhere from 5 to 30 percent before you even hear about it.

It is not at all inconceivable that, while your broker is urging you to buy, others higher up in the brokerage firm are advising their clients to sell.

As a hard and fast rule, a "buy" recommendation that comes to you in printed form from a brokerage firm should be a signal for you to pass on that offer. The stock has already been discovered, everyone's already in it, and you'd just be paying a premium price for it. In fact, the stock might be coming from another client of the same firm who's cashing in his profit. Once that kind of selling begins, you're suddenly sitting with a loss. To my intense embarrassment, that very thing happened to a close friend of mine whose account I had assigned to another broker in my firm because I had become too busy to properly look after it.

Unless you personally know a truly expert broker, or are related to one, your chances of getting a real insider to represent you are virtually nil—excepting if you happen to have $100,000 or more to invest. Anything less than that and there's just not that much in it for the broker.

Let's assume you have $10,000 to invest. The commission on that amount of money would be about $200, of which your broker would net 30 to 40 percent, about $60 to $80. If he gives your investments a chance, and does no more trading for you for a year, the $60 to $80 is the extent of his earnings on your account. How much attention can you expect for that kind of money? Even if you were to turn your portfolio over three times within a year, the commission would still come to less than $300 a year for the broker. If he's a good salesman, he's earning at least $30,000 a year, which means that your account represents less than 1 percent of his business.

Your broker can be a very smart person, but that doesn't help you if he's not focusing on your needs; and this is the real problem. Brokers are constantly thinking about other things than what is best for every client. One of my own brokers, a former lawyer and a very smart man, tells the story of how he managed to lose $5,000 for a doctor. Several times the doctor's account went down to $2,000 because of poor investments, but because this broker was a good salesman he managed to keep the account open. Finally, borrowing fifty percent of the money on margin, he bought a stock at six that went down to three, which wiped out the doctor's account. It wasn't that the broker was malicious. He was simply doing other things. The kind of money the doctor had invested was not important to him.

I don't care how hard we brokers try, we have a conflict of interest with our clients. I'm no exception. I'd love to have your business; I make money every time you trade. But even I, wanting you to make money as I do, could not represent your interests as well as you would like me to—or could represent them yourself. Unless you're bringing me an account with hundreds of thousands of dollars, you're going to do poorly in the competition for my attention. I've got to attend to my major clients first; if I don't, I lose them. And then there's my own account, which interests me more than anything.

As a small investor, you can't afford to fight this battle. If you're doing it now, you may be making some money. But you're sizably diminishing your chances of making substantial money and you're greatly increasing your chances of getting hurt.

Follow the Leader: A Losing Game on Wall Street

The most damning judgment of all against stockbrokers and the firms that manage money is that they don't do a good job of what they're primarily supposed to do—which is to find you good investments.

If your account has been with one of the big brokerage firms or investment management firms during the last five years, the chances are that you've lost a lot of money. The reason for this is simple: all of the big firms tend to follow the same major strategies, and five years ago all were committed to the idea that the way to make money in the stock market was to invest in the fifty biggest corporations.

Their reasoning was simple. They were investing big quantities of money, as much as $10 billion apiece; it seemed logical to them that big money ought to be invested in the biggest companies. Such companies, they believed, would be better managed, they would profit from the efficiencies of size, they would dominate their markets, and so forth.

On paper, the idea wasn't bad; there certainly were—and are—some outstanding values among the "nifty fifty." But there are two enormous problems inherent in such an undertaking that almost doom this strategy.

First, when so many people are following the same companies the stock in those companies is in such demand that it becomes expensive; you get in at a price that's very high relative to the value you're getting.

Second, such collective action is deceptive. It tends to support stocks at very high levels. What is really happening is that the buyers are all propping up one another's judgments. Once one of them begins to sell the stocks all of them had been buying, others follow suit, and support for the stocks collapses.

This "Blue Chip" theory of investing has always been popular because the argument for it seems to be so strong. After all, the biggest wouldn't be the biggest if they weren't also the best. Furthermore, runs the argument, the biggest will never go out of business, so you'll never lose your money.

It's unlikely that you'll lose all of your money if you buy Blue Chip stocks, but you could lose a lot of it if you buy them at the wrong price. Because so many people are aware of the Blue Chips, and because demand for their stocks is so persistent, they almost never sell at bargain prices. As a consequence, all kinds of investors have bought the Blue Chips at the wrong price. Eastman Kodak, which sold well above $100 a share for years, is now in the $40 to $50 range. General Motors, which reached $113 a share in the early sixties, has been below $30 and was still under $60 in late 1978. Even IBM, everybody's darling, has gone nowhere in the last 10 years, despite the fact that its earnings have continued to rise.

The Blue Chip theory is only one of several theories that come into vogue on Wall Street every now and then. Every one of these theories has had its day, and still has its exponents. Every one of them, in my opinion, is no longer valid. But if you're investing through a major brokerage house, you may be in thrall to these theories. Let's take them one by one.

The Growth Stock Theory:

The idea here is that you buy only stocks with a growth rate above a certain amount—say 12 to 15 percent per year. Given that continuous growth rate, the theory holds, the price of the stock cannot help but continue to rise.

The problem with the Growth Stock theory is twofold. First, past earnings are no guarantee of future earnings, even though they suggest a company that's vigorous. Second, as companies get bigger their growth rate tends to slow; they will continue to grow, but at a reduced rate. The reduced rate may be perfectly acceptable in economic terms, but if the market interprets a reduction in growth rate as a sign of weakness, and the market almost invariably does, the price of a company's stock will diminish.

THE LAMENTABLE RECORD OF THE BLUE CHIPS

1974-1978

Rank—% Price Change *

	Last Week	%	Last 13 Weeks	%	Last 26 Weeks	%	Year-To-Date	%	Last 5 Years *	%
	Dow Jones Ind.	-1.9	Dow Jones Ind.	-9.4	Dow Jones Ind.	-4.0	Dow Jones Ind.	-2.9	Dow Jones Ind.	-5.1
1	Sears, Roebuck	5.6	Exxon	7.0	Minn Mng Mfg	12.3	Minn Mng Mfg	22.7	Unit Technols	225.3
2	Goodyear Tire	4.1	Std Oil Cal	6.7	Eastman Kodak	8.7	Std Oil Cal	17.4	Johns Manville	57.6
3	Alcoa	1.1	Am Tel & Tel	-.8	Dupont Corp	6.2	Eastman Kodak	15.9	Am Brands	49.2
4	Gen Electric	1.0	Minn Mng Mfg	-2.5	Std Oil Cal	4.9	Am Brands	11.9	Am Can	36.7
5	Intl Paper	.6	Alcoa	-2.9	Intl Harvester	4.7	Intl Harvester	11.2	Gen Foods	31.6
6	Minn Mng Mfg	.0	Inco Ltd	-4.6	Exxon	3.9	Unit Technols	7.7	Intl Harvester	30.6
7	Bethlehem Stl	.0	Dupont Corp	-5.2	Gen Foods	2.5	Exxon	3.6	Std Oil Cal	30.4
8	Unit Technols	-.3	Proct & Gambl	-5.6	Proct & Gambl	.0	Dupont Corp	2.6	Owens-Illinois	25.5
9	Owens-Illinois	-.6	Intl Paper	-7.7	Am Tel & Tel	-1.8	Am Tel & Tel	.0	Gen Motors	22.8
10	Woolworth FW	-.7	Gen Foods	-8.4	Intl Paper	-2.1	Gen Foods	-.8	Esmark	22.5

Rank										
11	Westinghouse	−.7	Woolworth FW	−8.6	Alcoa	−2.4	Proct & Gambl	−1.6	Am Tel & Tel	19.2
12	Am Tel & Tel	−.8	Union Carbide	−8.9	Am Brands	−2.8	Woolworth FW	−2.0	Exxon	6.0
13	Union Carbide	−1.0	Am Brands	−9.2	Inco Ltd	−5.3	Alcoa	−2.4	Union Carbide	5.5
14	Am Brands	−1.3	Goodyear Tire	−9.2	Goodyear Tire	−6.6	Gen Electric	−2.8	Goodyear Tire	4.9
15	Johns Manville	−1.4	Texaco	−10.2	Texaco	−7.5	Intl Paper	−4.6	Woolworth FW	.7
16	Proct & Gambl	−1.5	Eastman Kodak	−10.9	Owens-Illinois	−7.7	Bethlehem Stl	−4.7	Alcoa	−6.3
17	Texaco	−1.6	Allied Chemical	−12.2	Esmark	−8.0	Westinghouse	−6.9	Proct & Gambl	−8.2
18	Am Can	−1.7	Sears, Roebuck	−12.3	Woolworth FW	−8.1	Goodyear Tire	−7.3	US Steel Corp	−9.3
19	Std Oil Cal	−1.9	Gen Motors	−13.4	Bethlehem Stl	−8.5	Am Can	−7.4	Intl Paper	−19.7
20	US Steel Corp	−2.7	Intl Harvester	−13.5	Gen Electric	−8.7	Inco Ltd	−8.0	Texaco	−21.3
21	Eastman Kodak	−2.7	Gen Electric	−13.6	Chrysler Cp.	−9.0	Gen Motors	−9.9	Dupont Corp	−22.3
22	Dupont Corp	−3.3	Owens-Illinois	−13.9	Gen Motors	−10.1	Union Carbide	−12.2	Gen Electric	−23.0
23	Allied Chemical	−3.8	Am Can	−16.3	Union Carbide	−10.8	Texaco	−16.7	Minn Mng Mfg	−23.7
24	Gen Foods	−3.9	Johns Manville	−19.1	Am Can	−12.0	Westinghouse	−18.8	Westinghouse	−33.5
25	Esmark	−3.9	Esmark	−19.4	Westinghouse	−14.0	Chrysler Cp.	−18.9	Chrysler Cp.	−35.2
26	Intl Harvester	−4.3	US Steel Corp	−19.5	Sears, Roebuck	−14.5	Owens-Illinois	−19.8	Allied Chemical	−36.0
27	Inco Ltd	−4.6	Chrysler Cp	−19.8	Unit Technols	−15.1	Johns Manville	−20.0	Bethlehem Stl	−39.0
28	Exxon	−5.5	Bethlehem Stl	−20.7	US Steel Corp	−16.5	Sears, Roebuck	−23.7	Sears, Roebuck	−46.7
29	Gen Motors	−6.8	Unit Technols	−23.7	Johns Manville	−20.6	US Steel Corp	−27.8	Eastman Kodak	−48.9
30	Chrysler Cp	−10.0	Westinghouse	−31.1	Allied Chemical	−27.0	Allied Chemical	−29.1	Inco Ltd	−55.3

* Ranked from end of Year 5 Years Ago and Into Current Year

Source: Dec. 4, 1978. Reprinted by permission of the *M/G Financial Weekly*

This doesn't mean that we don't like to buy stocks whose growth rate has been excellent and where we think this is going to continue. But one cannot use the growth rate alone to justify paying prices which are many times the earnings of a company. To pay multiples of earnings commensurate with that growth rate, as managers of investment portfolios are sometimes prone to do, has proven to be disastrous. Those who have done this have reasoned that if a company was growing at a rate of 20 percent a year, they could afford to pay twenty times the amount of its earnings per share of stock; if the growth was 30 percent a year, they could pay thirty times the amount of its earnings per share. The problem with this should be immediately evident. Once the growth rate slackened—as it inevitably must when a company reaches a certain size—the multiple immediately dropped, and the price of the stock with it.

When in the early 1960s Xerox came to market with its famous copying maching, its stock was selling below $2 a share. As the machine gained popularity, the price of the stock rose dramatically, Brokers and their clients were willing to pay 30 and 40 times the earnings-per-share for shares of Xerox. In 1972, the stock reached an all-time high of $171⅞—earnings that year were $3.24 a share—fifty-three times earnings. Then the growth rate slackened. By 1978, the stock had dropped as low as $40 a share.

I was once an exponent of the Growth Stock theory. In 1972 I recommended to my clients that they buy an insurance company stock that was selling at $80 a share. The company had a growth rate of 30 percent a year, and everything indicated that it would continue to grow at 30 percent a year. But then the earnings fell apart, and the price of the stock fell from $80 to $2. The stock was worth far more than $2—it's now selling for $12—but panic selling by investors forced the price down to that level.

Needless to say, that one experience caused me to abandon the Growth Stock theory.

The Follow-the-Trend Theory:

The idea here is that when a stock is rising you should buy it because someone behind you will buy it from you at a higher price. The idea comes from a Wall Street maxim that says, "Buy the strong performers, sell the weak ones."

The trouble with this theory is that you're paying more for the stock than the man in front of you, in the hope that the rising trend will continue. In a strong bull market this kind of strategy will often make you a lot of money in the short term, but sooner or later you're bound to lose, because the trend will eventually change. The market never goes straight up.

If you had bought on the trend of six years ago, most of your capital would be gone today. Most of the trend-watchers I know invariably buy high and sell low. That's a trend in itself, but one we want to avoid.

The Random Walk Theory:

This theory is one beloved by the stock market's intellectuals. It argues that every stock is selling at its correct price at any given time, and there's no way you can do better than average by buying stocks. It's as though you threw darts at the stock market tables and bought the ones you hit. You would do as well with those stocks, holds the Random Walk theory, as you would in the market as a whole.

I love intellectuals. I suppose I'm one myself. But this theory is so ludicrous that I have difficulty even discussing it. It leaves everything to chance in a game that ought to be played with arithmetic precision. It flies in the face of proof that there are investors who always do better—and worse—than the market.

Most of Wall Street's theories are little more than excuses

to justify the purchase of overvalued securities. Without such purchases, brokers couldn't stay in business.

But the real problem with Wall Street is more than a matter of its theories. It's a matter of Wall Street's own economics—which preclude the very kind of analysis and underwriting effort that would most benefit the small investor.

Wall Street's Cardinal Sin

The name of the game in investing is "information." Find a profitable company before the crowd does. Buy shares in the company for your clients and yourself. Then spread the word, and watch the price go up as other investors come in.

There are people who make a profession of finding profitable situations. They are known as "security analysts." I count myself among them. I'm afraid I don't have much that's good to say about my own profession.

Analysts are supposed to precisely measure the real worth of a company, so that investors can buy and sell its stock at a proper price. But most analysts aren't really equipped to distinguish value from fashion. Like me, too many of them are gamblers at heart. They rely on their impressions more than on research. They are seduced by earnings and tend to forget about value. In writing their reports on companies, they are too often influenced by what other analysts have written about those companies; on occasion, the report they use has, unbeknownst to them, been monitored, managed, or even partially written by the very company it purports to judge.

Analysts must write about companies to make their living. But often the companies will not give them access to the premises unless the analysts agree to let the companies review their reports prior to publication. The companies are then in a position to "dissuade" the analysts from any negative impressions.

The analysts are disposed to believe in the company in any case. "Negative stories don't sell," a Wall Street axiom has it. Analysts are also salesmen; they live by their commissions. They make more money recommending that stocks be bought than that they be sold.

For all of·these reasons, analysts either don't dig deeply enough or don't convey with sufficient energy the negative facts they uncover about companies.

But the ultimate test for an analyst is performance—do his choices make happy customers—and on this basis it would appear that Wall Street, itself, doesn't feel that its analysts have done a good job in recent years. Today there are far fewer analysts working on "The Street" than there were five years ago, eloquent testimony to the fact that their recommendations over this period have not done well at all. They have tended to be over-optimistic just before a decline in prices, and over-pessimistic just before a rise. Once again, the deadly game of follow-the-leader.

I don't think it's the analysts' fault. I think their position in the Wall Street hierarchy dooms them to poor performance. Very few security analysts are their own bosses. Most of them either work for the big institutions, or sell their work to them. As a consequence, they're beholden to the money managers who direct them or pay their salaries. The realities compel them to follow the thinking trends of their employers. They rarely get a chance to follow their own disciplined formulas.

But far worse than this lack of opportunity to follow a personal conviction is that the realities of their business compel the analysts to recommend expensive stocks and pass up inexpensive ones.

"Expensive" and "inexpensive" have nothing to do with

comparative prices. A stock selling for $100 may be less expensive than one selling for $10 if what you're buying for each dollar has more value.

The great irony of Wall Street—its cardinal sin—is that it passes up the best investments because they don't pay a big enough commission!

One of the most vivid memories of my career is of the time I called on an institutional investor who had one of the biggest reputations on Wall Street, to see if I could interest him in buying a stock I had discovered. The stock was selling at $7 a share; its prospects were extraordinary. "We can't look at that stock," he said, "It has only half a million shares outstanding. The total value of the company is only three and a half million dollars." What he meant was that the amount of money his firm would make in management fees by owning shares in a company this size would not pay the firm for its time. Four years later, the stock had split several times, the value of the original shares was $70 per share—and the money manager could now afford to buy it for his customers because there was enough money in it for him!

Let's go through this one more time with another example, so that we'll be sure you understand what you're dealing with when you do business with Wall Street.

One of the greatest values I have ever come across in my 22 years as a broker is in a company we'll call Apple Insurance. (I don't want to use its real name because I don't want you running out to buy the stock when circumstances may have changed its outlook between my writing and your reading of this book.) We'll call it Apple because it's truly the apple of my eye; its prospects are so extraordinary that 30 percent of the money I invest for my clients is invested in shares of Apple.

Now obviously, it's in my interest to interest other money managers in a favorite stock once my own clients have secured their positions. In the case of Apple, the money managers would listen with special interest because my strong suit is the insurance business. But look at what happens.

Money Manager: It's too small.

Me: What do you mean, it's too small?

Money Manager: It's not big enough for us. It's only got a market value of $70 million.

Me: So what? The value's there.

Money Manager: We will not buy more than 5 percent of the stock of any one company. Five percent of $70 million is only $3.5 million. That's not big enough for us. Come back and see us when the market value's $100 million.

This same money manager will buy 5 percent of Company X with a market value of $120 million, even though the company is earning a fraction of what Apple's earning. The reason: He'll get fees on $6 million rather than on $3.5 million. He'll then put the shares of Company X into his clients' accounts. The prospects for profits for the clients are far, far greater with Apple—but the fees on the transaction with Company X are something the money manager can count on right now.

Time after time, the large institutions tell you that they can't "afford" to look at a company unless it has a market value of $100 million. The smaller institutions say they won't look at anything that has a market value of less than $20 million.

Analysts aren't paid to follow small companies—the very companies that can give you the greatest chance for profits— because there is not enough trading in the stock to generate sufficient commissions. If the analysts, and the firms they work for, were interested primarily in making money for their clients they would seek out these small companies. But that's not the way it works on Wall Street. Clients' profits are secondary; the primary concern is to cover the firm's overhead and generate a profit.

You can't blame your broker for wanting to make some money; if he doesn't, he'll go out of business. But that doesn't mean that you have to make less money than you could, or break even, or even lose money by serving your broker's self interest—if you have an alternative.

You do, and it's a beauty. You're going to discover these undiscovered companies. Small, profitable companies with brilliant futures. There are hundreds of them, undervalued, accessible, eager to tell their stories. You're going to learn how to find them and evaluate them and, finally, choose the ones most likely to turn your $10,000 into $100,000 in nine years.

CHAPTER 3
How to Beat the Crowd

Some years ago American Express had the misfortune to be indirectly involved, through one of its subsidiaries, in what came to be known as the Great Salad Oil scandal. The president of the subsidiary had been borrowing a great deal of money, using as collateral an enormous vat of salad oil that he maintained in New Jersey. One day, someone thought to climb the ladder of this vat to have a look inside. The vat was empty.

The moment the story broke, the stock of American Express came under severe selling pressure, even though the subsidiary represented an inconsequential portion of the company's business. Within a few months, the stock had dropped more than 40 percent. There was a certain logic to the reaction, apart from that connected with the potential legal liabilities involved; investors reasoned that the adverse publicity might cause consumers to lose confidence in American Express, in which case they might stop buying the world's best known travelers' checks. Merchants might even refuse to honor the American Express credit card.

Enter Warren Buffett, a young investor from the Middle West, then in his early thirties. Buffett did something so simple that for years thereafter other investors would anguish that they hadn't thought of it themselves.

First, Buffett bought some American Express travelers' checks. Then he presented the checks at a number of banks and business establishments. In every case, the checks were honored. Next, Buffett visited a series of stores and restaurants and presented his American Express card to pay his bills. Not a single proprietor challenged his card.

Buffett, who had made his tests at a time when the news about the scandal was at its peak, concluded that the problem the company was experiencing simply didn't make any difference in the long run. American Express was a profitable company with an enormous credibility among consumers. If the business was there, the company would survive, even if it had to settle a bunch of liability claims. So Warren Buffett quietly bought up 10 percent of American Express common stock at a time when no one else would touch it—and within two years had made several million dollars for himself and a handful of clients.

You don't have to be a professional investor to do what Warren Buffett did. Anyone could have done it. Incredible profits can be made, and often are, by the most commonsensical decisions and actions.

But the real moral of Warren Buffett's story is that to make significant money in common stocks you have to be a loner, making decisions that go against the crowd.

As 1978 drew to a close, the crowd was saying that the stock market was no place in which to have investments. For those who think of themselves as investors *in the market,* I would agree. They were getting mauled by the prevailing psychology. Because they think like the crowd, they were acting like the crowd—selling in a panic. When they eventually get back into the market, as they invariably do, you can be certain that they will be buying shares in which the professionals have already taken their position.

In bad times, investors tend to view everything negatively. In good times, they see everything through rose-tinted glasses. It follows, then, that the prices paid for securities are much lower in bad times than in good times. If you can find a solid company whose shares have been driven down by a general selling wave, you've got the perfect bargain.

I would have loved Shakespeare as a client; he would have made the ideal investor. "Sweet are the uses of adversity," he wrote. Every investor should pin those words on his wall.

What better proof is there of this maxim than Germany and Japan after World War II? Where could there be a worse place to invest, in theory, than in two countries wasted by war? Even as late as the early 1960s the same values could have been bought for a tenth of the price in Japan that they were selling for on the New York Stock Exchange. Today, Germany and Japan are the most prosperous industrial societies in the world.

It's the irreverent iconoclast who gets the bargains, regardless of what the market does. The maxim holds even in the case of individual stocks. If everyone likes a particular stock, it's going to sell at a high price in relation to its values; as more and more people learn about the stock, the higher the price becomes. But when a company is completely out of favor, that's the time its stock price may be ridiculously low in relation to its value.

Consider the case of Government Employees Insurance Company, known on The Street as GEICO. GEICO's business is the sale of automobile insurance. For years the company had done a volume business at preferential rates. Its stock, which had once sold as low as 28 cents a share, rose to $60. Then word got around that GEICO had a backlog of unpaid claims, far greater than its management had anticipated. The stock began to plummet. On the day that *Time* and *Newsweek* came out with stories suggesting that the company was about to go out of business, the price of the stock fell to $2. Everyone was dumping the stock—brokers, analysts, and investors.

The stories of GEICO's demise made absolutely no sense to me. There was not a single month in which the company didn't have more cash coming in than going out. It had applied for and received substantial rate increases, which meant that future premiums would be more than enough to offset claims. Moreover, GEICO had liquid assets of half a billion dollars.

When the stock hit $4 a share, I began to buy large blocks of it for my clients, and I kept buying it as it fell to $2 a share. Within a year most of my clients had doubled their money, and some had tripled it. Eventually the stock rose to $10 a share, and then sold off—by which point my clients were out.

But you don't need periods of stress, either with the market or with individual stocks, to make this kind of money. You can do it simply by discovering a promising company.

A Fantasy Come True

The great dream of every investor is to find a stock before anyone else—one that's selling for peanuts relative to its worth—and then have the rest of the world discover it. Let me tell you how that fantasy became reality for me. Keep in mind as we proceed that what happened was not so esoteric that it couldn't also happen to you.

In 1972 I met an old friend of mine at a party, a young doctor specializing in gynecology. He told me about a visit he'd received that week from a salesman for a New England company called Dynatech, which manufactured medical products. One of those products had fascinated him because it would enable him to make a simple office procedure out of an operation that had previously required hospitalization. He'd bought the product, my friend said, and he was sure that doctors all over the country would buy it as well. He suggested that I look into Dynatech as a possible investment.

I called the company's president in Boston. Luckily, he

was coming to New York. We met at the Plaza Hotel for a drink. Dynatech, he told me, had begun modestly in 1959 with just a few employees. In the 13 years since, it had managed to develop a number of useful products in addition to the one I'd heard about. There were now 75 employees, and sales were around $7 million a year.

What impressed me most was that I was the first analyst this man had ever talked to. Here was a rock-solid company with a sizable future and absolutely no publicity about its products, achievements, or prospects. Although its stock was being traded in the over-the-counter market, it had never been promoted by any Wall Street firm. Only two Wall Street brokers were making a market in its securities.

So I began to buy the stock at $7 a share, and I continued buying when the stock fell all the way to $3 a share. Over the next year, I accumulated 15,000 shares.

And then what I had hoped for came to pass. Others heard about Dynatech and began to write reports. The reports coincided with a healthy increase in earnings. In the next four years, sales went over $20 million, a threefold increase, and the price of the stock rose with them.

The only mistake I ever made in Dynatech was to sell half my shares when the stock hit $19. By 1978, six years after my original purchase, my shares were worth $70, ten times what I had paid for them. But the sale had paid off my initial investment, and I was still sitting with profits of half a million dollars.

Now let's be realistic. Presidents of companies love to talk to analysts. They'll give them all the time they want. A favorable report on their company by an analyst is exactly what they're looking for; it drives up the price of their stock. As original shareholders, they stand to profit more than anyone.

But, what the president of Dynatech told me was exactly

what you would have been told had you called blind and spoken to that person in the corporation whose job it is to talk to prospective stockholders. I promise you that I learned no special secrets on that day in New York that prompted my investment.

A Plethora of Treasures

There are 5,000 companies whose securities are traded on the major stock exchanges and the over-the-counter market. At least a fifth of these companies are either undiscovered or else have been forgotten after once having been discovered.

There are another 6,000 companies in the United States whose stock prices can be ascertained by consulting special financial publications. Many of these companies are also undiscovered.

Not every one of these several thousand companies is a potential Dynatech. But hundreds among them are.

Why haven't these companies been found by the professionals? One reason is that the market is inefficient. Poor communications and differing perceptions of values result in inefficient pricing of securities. Remember Oscar Wilde's famous observation? "A fool is a man who knows the price of everything and the value of nothing." On the basis of what goes on in the stock market, it would appear that there are many fools investing, because the prices of stocks in relation to the values of those stocks are all askew.

An even more suggestive reason as to why so many promising companies go undiscovered is one we've already seen. The heavyweight investors can't be bothered with companies whose market value doesn't meet their standards. And, by definition, no small company's market value does. The biggest brokerage house can't afford to pay their analysts to follow these companies because there's not enough of these companies' stock selling at a high enough price to generate sufficient commissions. Ironically, the lower the stock trades—and the greater its value in relation to its price—the less inclined are the analysts to follow it because there's even less of a commission in the trading.

What an advantage this gives the small investor! Wall Street's commission-oriented business operation automatically eliminates a good portion of his competition. Given the fact that the small investor is—or ought to be—looking for long-term investments, the competition shrinks still further because brokers favor the short term investments that bring them more commissions.

The small investor has yet another advantage. His activity almost never dislocates the price of the stock he's trying to buy.

When you invest $10,000 in a stock, little or nothing happens to the market. If you wanted to buy more the next day, you could probably buy it for the same price. But when a big institution comes around with a million dollars, it's bound to affect the price of the stock to the institution's own disadvantage. Its own activity pushes up the price of the stock. True, the first shares it bought are now worth more, but that's only because of the institution's own demand. Once the demand has slackened, the stock could slip back to the price of the shares originally bought by the institution.

The smaller the pool of dollars you work with, the better your chances of capitalizing on such opportunities. By the ancient law of supply and demand, if you're going into the market in a big way, your own activity will push up the price.

Carl Mason: From $200 to $2 Million

To see what can happen when you invest for yourself, let's consider the case of a man we'll call Carl Mason.

Carl is in his late thirties. I had known him only slightly before 1973, but got to know him well during those frantic weeks when Equity Funding was falling apart. Carl had been an administrator at Equity Funding, but he had resigned from the company after learning of its irregular business practices. Without his help, I couldn't have exposed the fraud.

Carl is a great example of a man who invests with no conflict of interest. He represents only himself. No broker is pressing him to buy and sell securities; when he does trade, he simply gives his order to one or more brokerage houses, my own among them. But he doesn't trade very often. He's a long-term investor. When he buys a stock, it's with the intention of holding it for years. If his judgment was right to begin with, he reasons, the company will continue to grow. Then, of course, there's the matter of taxes; if he sold a stock as soon as he had a large profit in his securities, his tax would be enormous. Carl Mason's is one of the best success stories I know.

Starting with a few hundred dollars, Carl had run his net worth up to $150,000 by the time I met him. Five years later, his net worth had risen to $2 million, all of it made in common stocks.

Carl's methods differ from mine in certain respects, but as far as the fundamentals go, they're exactly the same. Basically, he looks for undiscovered, undervalued companies. He gets in ahead of the crowd, knowing that someone will eventually find out about the stock, buy a lot of it, and raise the price of his shares. If individuals don't find the company, other companies will. One of Carl's best investments was a company called Deseret Pharmaceutical. He bought the company's stock at $5 a share at the end of 1974; two years later, Deseret was taken over by Warner-Lambert at a price of $38 a share.

Eventually, all companies get discovered. It's a question of who discovers them first.

This is the point at which you might be saying, "That's

swell, Dirks, but how? What chance have I got against the professionals?"

Until a few years ago, you wouldn't have had much chance. Today you have every chance in the world. Part of the change goes back to Equity Funding; since the exposure of the fraud and subsequent get-tough policy by federal regulators, corporations have been far more willing, even eager, to disclose information to stockholders and prospective stockholders.

The second development that puts you on an even footing with the professionals is your ready access to a vital investment tool used in the past only by professionals—a highly significant number, once hard to come by, that appears now in your daily newspaper.

Together, these two elements can give you the clues you need in your search for hidden corporate treasures.

CHAPTER 4
Earnings Yield: The Missing Clue

Suppose I called you to suggest that you buy a stock, you asked me how much of a return you'd be getting on your money, and I told you 4 percent.

"Are you kidding?" you'd reply. "Why on earth would I want to risk my money in the stock market for a return of 4 percent? I can get 5 percent at the bank with no risk at all."

If you've been an investor in the past, it's going to come as a shock to you to learn that, in all probability, you've made some investments in stocks that have earned you 4 percent— or even less.

What we're talking about is "earnings yield." In spite of the fact that it's the most relevant, nay, indispensable information an investor should have before he makes an investment, the concept of earnings yield is scarcely known in the United States.

A while back our firm prepared an advertisement stressing that we had stocks for sale with earnings yields of 40 percent. The ad was sent to the New York Stock Exchange for approval. Shortly thereafter we got a call from a representative of the exchange. "You can't run that ad," he told us.

"Why not?"

"Well," the representative admitted reluctantly, "we've never heard of earnings yield."

If the Stock Exchange had never heard of earnings yield, he argued, the investor probably hadn't either—a respectable point. So we ran the ad with an asterisk next to the term and a footnote explaining what earnings yield was.

Earnings yield is the percentage of what the company earns each year per share, based on the price you paid for it. If you buy a stock at $10 a share and it earns $4 a share you have an earnings yield of 40 percent. That doesn't mean that you get 40 percent in cash. It means that the company's value in relation to your purchase price goes up 40 percent that year.

When was the last time your broker told you what would be the earnings yield of a stock he wanted you to buy? The chances are he's never used the term, because he's never heard of it.

Yet almost all investors, no matter how unsophisticated, know what the price/earnings (P/E) ratio is. A stock earning $1 a year and selling for $10 a share is said to have a price/ earnings ratio of ten to one.

What most investors—and many brokers—don't know is that the true significance of that ratio is understood only when you take its reciprocal.

The reciprocal is calculated by dividing the price/earnings ratio into 100. That gives you the earnings yield.

When a stock is selling at five times earnings, it means its 10 percent earnings yield is 20 percent.

There were times during the go-go days of the early 1960s when brokers would advise their clients to buy stock selling at fifty times earnings. And there were plenty of clients who bought those stocks without realizing that their new investment was earning 2 *percent*. In such cases, the investor could sell at a profit only if the public was foolish enough to bid up the price of the stock even further.

We've seen the dark side of this equation. Now let's move toward daylight.

When a stock is selling at seven times earnings, that means it's earning a little more than 14 percent. Not bad.

When a stock is selling at six times earnings, that means an earnings yield of 16.6 percent. Still better.

When a stock is selling at five times earnings, the yield is 20 percent.

Four times earnings, 25 percent.

Three times earnings, 33 percent.

Two times earnings, 50 percent.

Let's put aside for the moment the question of *why* stocks might be selling for so little in relation to their earnings. Let's just work on the idea of why stocks that sell at low multiples of their earnings are better buys than others selling at much higher multiples.

The Magic of Compound Interest

You're undoubtedly familiar with the term compound interest. Your bank has explained it to you when pitching a savings account to you. Or you've learned about it when you invested in government bonds. There's nothing new about the idea—the interest earns interest in turn. What you may not be familiar with is the spectacular result that occurs when, instead of having your investment compound at 5 percent at the bank, it compounds at 14 percent or even more in a common stock investment.

Money invested at 5 percent compound interest doubles every 14.2 years.

Money invested at 14 percent compound interest doubles every 5.29 years.

To calculate how long it takes your money to double at any given compound interest rate, just use the "Rule of 72," one of those little mathematical tricks, which calls for dividing the interest rate into 72. Thus, a rate of 25 percent compound interest would double your money in just under three years, a rate of 33 percent, in just over two years.

But to fully appreciate the magic of compound interest, let's make a few extensions.

First, $10,000 invested at 5 percent

Year 1	$10,500
Year 5	$12,800
Year 10	$16,300
Year 20	$26,500

Next $10,000 invested at 15 percent

Year 1	$11,500
Year 5	$20,100
Year 10	$40,500
Year 20	$163,700

Next $10,000 invested at 20 percent

Year 1	$12,000
Year 5	$24,900
Year 10	$61,900
Year 20	$383,400

Next $10,000 invested at 33 percent

Year 1	$13,300
Year 5	$41,615
Year 10	$173,187
Year 20	$2,999,389

Is there anyone out there who wouldn't be content with an investment of $10,000 that became $2,999,389 in 20 years? That is exactly what you'd have if you invested $10,000 in a company selling at three times earnings, and if, each year thereafter, the earnings yield of 33 percent was reflected in the price of the stock. (We're assuming that management would continue to reinvest the earnings in the best possible manner.)

The way to beat inflation today is to compound your money at a rate higher than the 7 percent after-tax return that

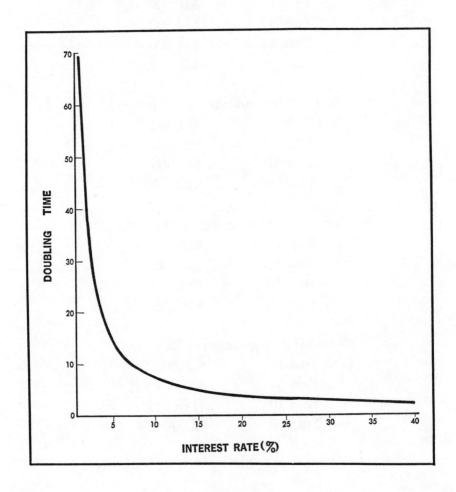

would barely keep you even. Your objective ought to be to find companies with earnings yields that give you the dramatic appreciation of the examples above.

But Where's the Money?

At this point you might be saying, "Wait a minute, Dirks, what do you mean I'm earning 20 percent? I see that the stock is earning 20 percent of the amount it's selling for, but I'm not getting paid anything. So how can I be *earning* 20 percent?"

If the company were to pay out all of its earnings in the form of a dividend at the end of the year, you'd have no doubts about earning 20 percent. You paid $10 a share for the stock, the stock earned $2 a share, and you received $2 for every share you owned. That can happen—corporations do occasionally pay dividends equal to their per share earnings—but that's not what we're looking for, because a successful company with good prospects will reinvest most or all of the earnings in the business so that it can continue to grow. Just because the company doesn't distribute the earnings doesn't mean they're not there; they're simply being held for reinvestment. When that happens the value of what you bought increases by the amount of the earnings.

Now, what if the opposite happens and no one takes notice? That can happen, particularly at a time when a selling

Now this increase in the value of your investment should be reflected in the price of the stock. As the earnings rise, as the value of the company increases, the stock should sell for more because it's now worth more than it was. Usually, that's what happens. That stock you bought for $10 when it was earning $2 a share should increase to $20 if the earnings increase to $4 a share. Just that amount of increase in the price of the stock would be justified to maintain the five to one ratio of price to earnings. Often however, an increase in earnings of that magnitude is celebrated by a disproportionate increase in the price of the stock. Investors say, "Hey, this company's terrific. Look how much its earnings have increased." As they rush in to buy the stock, their demand pushes up the price.

Now what if the opposite happens and no one takes notice? That can happen, particularly at a time when a selling panic occurs, as was the case in the fall of 1978. While the price of the stock doesn't rise in proportion to the increase in its earnings, you have the satisfaction of knowing that your earnings yield has increased. If the price of the stock remains at $10 a share even though earnings have risen to $4 a share, you now have a 40 percent yield on your investment—a signal for you to buy all the stock you can.

Theoretically, the stock could keep selling at $10 a share even if the earnings increased to $10 a share. But the likelihood of that happening on both historical and mathematical grounds is virtually impossible. There are just too many knowing investors around looking for value to permit the stock to remain dormant; once they start to buy the stock its price has to rise.

But let's say, just for the exercise, that they don't find the stock. What then? With all the money that it's earning at its disposal, the corporation would be eager to reduce the amount of shares outstanding; so the corporation buys up its own shares—which raises the price. Why shouldn't it buy its own shares? It would be earning 100 percent on its money, and would not even have to pay any tax.

So, you see, there really is a relationship between price and value. People will pay more for a stock with greater value, just as they'll pay more for a Cadillac than they will for a Chevrolet.

Lucky Seven, Unlucky Thirteen

Tell an investor that a stock has a price/earnings ratio of 7 and it could pass right over his head. But tell him that he'll earn 14 percent on his money and you've got yourself an audience.

Fourteen percent—which is the growth you get when you invest in a stock selling at seven times earnings—is the least return you ought to get for risking your money.

Why 14 percent? Why seven to one?

A 14 percent return is 4 to 5 percent more than you could make by investing your money in bonds, which have almost no risk, and 3 to 4 percent more than you could make investing in second deeds of trust, which have some risk, but not as much as common stocks. If other investments with little or no risk began yielding 14 percent, obviously that return would no longer be sufficient inducement for the extra risk inherent in a common stock investment. But right now, it is.

When we look for common stock investments, therefore, the first thing we want to know is the price/earnings ratio. We automatically eliminate any stock selling at more than seven times its earnings.

Lucky seven, unlucky thirteen.

Keep those numbers in mind and you'll never go wrong.

Any stock that's selling at seven times earnings or less is a candidate for a buy. Its earnings yield will be 14 percent or more.

Any stock with an earnings yield of 13 or less, it follows, would be eliminated as a prospect.

You don't even have to know how to calculate the reciprocal of the price/earnings ratio so long as you understand its significance. Because that's the tool once used almost exclusively by professionals that's now so accessible to you.

Please see the sample stock table from the New York Stock Exchange. The magic number appears in the column headed P-E (price/earnings).

SAMPLE STOCK TABLE FROM THE NEW YORK STOCK EXCHANGE

12 Month High	12 Month Low		Yld.	P-E	Sales in 100s	High	Low	Close	Net Chg.
				— A —					
39½	28⅞	ACF 2.10	6.8	7	61	31	30⅞	30⅞	– ¼
23⅝	15½	AMF 1.24	7.8	7	311	16	15¾	16	– ⅛
14¾	8⅞	APL 1	10.7	13	82	9½	9¼	9⅜	....
48⅜	32⅜	ARA 1.64	4.5	8	257	36⅞	36⅛	36⅛	– ⅞
31⅜	19	ASA 1	4.1	...	540	24¾	24⅛	24½	– ⅜
14⅞	8⅛	ATO .48	5.1	4	59	9½	9	9⅜	– ¼
40	29	AbbtLb .84	2.7	13	773	31½	30¾	30⅞	– ¾
23¾	11⅞	AcmeC 1	6.1	6	21	17	16½	16½	– ½
6¼	3	AdmDg .04	1.1	5	16	3⅞	3⅝	3⅝	– ⅛
13	11¼	AdàEx 1.11e	9.4	...	74	12	11¾	11¾	– ⅜
8½	3⅞	AdmMI .20e	4.3	7	14	4¾	4⅝	4⅝	– ¼
32⅞	13⅜	Addrsg .28	1.4	8	254	20⅛	19½	19¾	– ⅜
45¾	31	AetnaLf 2.20	6.0	4	450	36¾	36⅛	36½	+ ¼
15	12⅛	Aguirre	....	32	25	13¼	13	13⅛	– ⅜
26¾	15⅞	Ahmans 1	5.4	4	x317	19	18⅝	18⅝	– ⅜
4	2¼	Aileen	....	...	27	2½	2½	2½	....
31⅞	22½	AirPrd .60	2.4	9	260	25¼	25	25	– ¼
26¾	14	AirbFrt 1	5.5	10	25	18¼	18⅛	18¼	....
15¼	11¼	Akzona .80	6.9	13	20	11⅝	11⅝	11⅝	....
18	14¾	AlaGas 1.40	9.4	6	7	15⅛	14⅞	14⅞	– ⅛
9¾	8	AlaPd pf .87	10.3	...	16	8½	8⅜	8½	+ ⅛
99½	85	AlaP pf 9	10.3	...	z110	87	86½	87	+ 1¾
104½	90⅞	AlaP pf 9.44	9.7	...	z60	97	97	97	+ 1⅝
93	78	AlaP pf 8.28	10.5	...	z240	79	d77⅝	79	+ ⅞
22¼	13¼	Alaskin .66	3.9	15	347	17⅜	16⅜	16¾	– ¼
40	16	Albany 1	4.3	7	39	24½	23½	23½	– 1¼
9⅞	6¼	Alberto .36	5.4	9	120	7⅛	6⅝	6⅝	– ⅜
46¾	24⅞	Albertsn .96	3.0	8	83	32¾	31¾	31¾	– 1¼
37	21⅝	AlcanA 2	6.2	5	326	32⅜	32	32⅛	....
31⅜	21½	AlcoStd 1.16	5.0	5	88	23¾	22¾	23¼	– ¾
8½	5¼	Alexdr .40	7.6	6	150	5⅝	5¼	5¼	– ⅜
26	13⅝	AllgCp 1	5.3	7	37	19	18¾	18⅞	– ⅜
15	3⅝	AllegAir	....	2	523	8⅛	7⅛	7½	– ⅝
29¼	18	Allg pf 1.87	9.7	...	38	20¼	19¼	19¼	– ¾

20¼	13¾	AllgLd 1.28	8.5	7	66	15⅝	15	15	– ⅝
38⅜	32	AllgL pf 3	9.3	...	5	32⅛	32	32⅛	– ⅛
23⅞	20⅛	AllgL pr 2.19	10.1	...	32	21⅝	21½	21⅝	....
21⅞	16½	AllgPw 1.72	10.3	9	130	16¾	16⅝	16¾	....
19⅝	13⅛	AllenGp 1	7.1	6	58	14⅝	13⅜	14⅛	– ⅜
35	20⅞	Allergan .50	2.1	12	27	24¾	24¼	24¼	– ¾
45⅝	30⅜	AlldCh 2	6.6	7	437	31	d30¼	30⅜	– ⅝
15½	9⅞	AlldMnt .80	7.6	7	36	10⅝	10¼	10½	– ⅛
16¾	12⅝	AlldPd .60	4.4	...	16	13⅝	13½	13½	– ⅛
28	18⅝	AlldStr 1.40	6.0	6	296	23⅝	23½	23½	....
3	⅝	viAlldSup	....	...	476	⅞	¾	⅞	– ⅛
38⅜	22⅛	AllisCh 1.50	5.2	5	659	29¾	28¾	28¾	– 1⅛
16⅞	8⅞	AllrAu .60b	5.1	8	6	12¼	11¾	11¾	– ¾
22¼	14½	AlphPr .72a	4.8	5	15	15⅜	15	15	– ⅛
53	38½	Alcoa 2	4.5	6	709	44⅞	44¼	44¼	– ¼
26	13⅞	AmlSug 1	7.0	14	66	14⅜	d13¾	14¼	+ ¼
53⅛	31	Amax 2.20	5.2	25	136	43¼	42½	42½	– ½
126¼	81	Amax pf 5.25	5.0	...	1	104	104	104	– 1¼

Unless you know what the price-earnings ratio is, reading a table like the one above is like trying to drive a car without an engine. In the 1960s when many stocks were selling at price/earnings ratios of twenty and thirty, there was a reason why none of the professionals wanted to advertise the point. The earning yields—which, remember, are the reciprocals of the P-E ratios—were downright embarrassing and not very marketable—5, 4, even 3 percent returns on your investment. Investments with such earnings yields were pure speculation; you were betting that earnings *might* increase—or that other investors would be even more foolish than you had been when you bought your stock, and drive the price up still further.

Ten years ago, when stocks were yielding an average of 6 percent, one almost had to speculate to make a lot of money. Today the price-earning ratios tell us that hundreds of stocks are yielding anywhere from 15 to 40 percent. Why speculate when you can earn that kind of money without much risk? It's silly to risk losing any capital at all.

We took a count at the close of the market on December 1, 1978, to see how many stocks fit into our 14-percent-or-better earnings yield category. On the New York Stock Exchange, there were 784 stocks with price-earnings ratios of seven to one or less. On the American Stock Exchange, there were 374 such stocks. So there were 1,185 potential candidates for investment, without even counting over-the-counter securities.

Low, Lower, Lowest = Good, Better, Best

Earnings represent what a company has made as a consequence of its activity over a period of 12 months. If a company is earning $2 a share, all things being equal, it should continue to earn at least $2 a share. If it doesn't earn that much, something is wrong. The company ought to be earning at least 7 percent more each year to qualify as a good investment; that amount would just accommodate inflation.

In addition to a high earnings yield, we're looking for a company that's increasing its earnings by 14 percent or more each year. A company that is increasing its earnings at 14 percent will double its earnings roughly every five years. If the price/earnings ratio remains constant, the price of the company's stock will double in that period. As we've already seen, that kind of steady performance is rewarded with increased attention by other buyers, and your profit is even greater.

Let's say you bought that stock earning $2 a share at three times earnings, or $6. If the earnings double over the five year period, and the price/earnings ratio remains the same, the price of the stock will rise to $12. But if other investors want to buy the stock, their demand for it could raise the price. Then, instead of selling at three times earnings, the stock might sell at six times earnings, or double its old price/earnings ratio. Your $6 stock would then be worth $24, four times what you paid for it.

The lower the price/earnings ratio of your stock, the more its price can be expected to rise. We can prove the point statistically. One study of stocks traded on the New York Stock Exchange showed that the 10 percent of stocks in the lowest price/earnings ratio category far outdistanced those in the highest category in a nine year period beginning in 1967. The perfomance was consistent from category to category; those in the lowest category did better than those in the next highest, and so forth.

But the study went even further. It showed that if an investor had switched his portfolio on a quarterly basis, kicking out stocks whose price/earnings ratios had risen in favor of those whose ratios had fallen, he would have enjoyed the highest possible return on his investment. By constantly maintaining a portfolio of stocks in the lowest 10 percent price/earnings ratio category, he would have gained $5 for every dollar he had invested—during a period, incidentally, when it wasn't easy to make profits in securities. If, conversely, he'd had the bad fortune to constantly switch into stocks in the highest price/earnings ratio category, each dollar he'd invested would have been worth only 84 cents after nine years.

What this means to you is that when you are monitoring five investments and one of them moves up smartly in price relative to its earnings, say six to one, you ought to consider selling that stock and replacing it with a new discovery that's selling at three to one. That kind of switching, or upgrading, might not be a good idea for tax purposes, but the theory is sound, nonetheless.

"All right, Dirks," you're saying now, "why, if a stock selling at three times earnings is such a better investment than a stock selling at seven times earnings, should I even bother with the stock selling at seven times earnings? Why shouldn't all my money be invested in stocks selling at three times earnings? Why make 14 percent on my money when I can make 33 percent on my money?"

Why the Institutions Didn't Make Money

Of the 75 companies most widely held by institutional investors, only 12 met our standard and 8 of those just barely. No wonder the institutions did poorly. The key column is at the right.

The answer is that you should invest in the stocks with the lower price/earnings ratios and larger earnings yields, all things being equal.

But sometimes all things aren't equal. A stock may be selling at only three times its earnings because of a fluke. This year the company had a tremendous rise in earnings because of an enormous government contract, but next year's going to be terrible. If, however, it looks like next year's going to be just as good as this you've found a great opportunity.

Me and P/E

If you're the average investor, you probably have a notion that your broker goes into the market to buy you 100 shares of a stock after you've decided you want it. That's the way it can work, but sometimes the broker is selling you stock from a supply already obtained by his firm—particularly if the stock is traded over the counter.

Because so many of the clients who trade with me give me discretion over their accounts, I automatically put them into stocks in which my firm takes a position. *Ninety-nine percent of the stocks I buy for my clients are selling at seven times earnings or less.* Except for extraordinary circumstances, it makes no sense whatever to buy any other kind of security.

Anyone who knew me before Equity Funding will recognize this change in my investment pattern as tantamount to a conversion.

Occasionally, I'll succumb to my old weakness for gambling, and speculate on a special situation. I know better, but I'm human. Sometimes I win, but other times I have the kind of experience that makes me vow once again never to get involved.

By and large, however, my work is directed toward one objective: switching into stocks with low price/earnings multiples.

In 1978, my firm was heavily invested in Hanover Insurance Company. When we first started buying the stock, it was earning $7 a share and selling for $19 to $21, or three times earnings. The stock got as high as $33 a share in 1978, or a little more than four times earnings, and then went back down to $21 in the great slide that fall. Selling the Hanover Insurance stock never occurred to me. To the contrary, I bought all I could get at that low price.

I'm not the only one playing this game. One day during the selling spree of October 1978 I got a call from John Templeton, the most successful manager of public mutual funds in the country. "I love buying stocks at three times earnings," he said, "but I'd like even better to buy stocks that are two times earnings five years from now." What Templeton was doing was adding a projection to current earnings. He had Hanover Insurance specifically in mind. The company's earnings five years from now are expected to be $16 a share. At the time of our conversation, Hanover was selling at $28 a share, less then two times its projected earnings five years hence. Assuming the price/earnings ratio of Hanover rises to more normal levels (a very safe assumption), the company's shares could be worth three, four, or even five times what we bought them for in the fall of 1978.

INSTITUTIONAL FAVORITES 1976/1977 (NYSE issues)

	Closing Price April 4, 1977	Institutional Holdings		Indicated Dividend Rate($)	Yield on Indicated Dividend (%)	Per Share Earnings Last 12 Months($)	P-E Ratio
		Companies	Shares (000)				
Int'l Business Machines ..	275¾	1,424	51,060	10.00	3.6	15.94	17
Exxon Corp..........	50⅝	943	131,907	3.00	5.9	5.90	8
American Tel & Tel	62⅝	893	79,052	4.20	6.7	6.27	9
Eastman Kodak........	67¾	852	49,961	2.10	3.1	4.03	16
General Motors........	66¾	855	73,492	5.55	8.3	10.08	6
General Electric........	48⅝	818	61,177	1.80	3.7	4.12	11
Xerox Corp...........	47⅝	670	34,233	1.20	2.5	4.51	10
Texaco, Inc..........	26¾	613	65,136	2.00	7.5	3.20	8
Sears, Roebuck & Co....	60⅜	573	32,783	2.10	3.5	4.37	13
Atlantic Richfield.......	52¼	506	35,672	1.60	3.1	5.04	10
Citicorp	27¾	541	50,900	1.06	3.8	3.24	8
Merck & Co	55	515	30,389	1.50	2.7	3.38	16
Mobil Corp...........	66¾	533	29,933	3.80	5.7	9.07	7
Dow Chemical........	37	533	54,861	1.00	2.7	3.30	11
Minnesota Mining & Mfg .	49½	501	36,327	1.70	3.4	2.94	16
Standard Oil (Ind.)......	51⅝	522	38,208	2.60	5.0	6.09	8
Ford Motor...........	53⅜	429	41,620	3.20	6.0	10.45	5
Union Carbide	55¼	452	19,716	2.80	5.1	7.15	7
Phillips Petroleum	55⅛	454	20,664	2.00	3.6	5.39	10
General Tel & Elect	29⅝	449	30,062	2.00	6.8	3.29	9
Kresge (S.S.)	32⅜	442	54,236	0.32	1.0	2.15	15
Burroughs Corp	60½	392	16,846	0.80	1.3	4.62	13
Gulf Oil	28¼	435	38,675	1.80	6.4	4.19	6
Amer Home Products	29¼	456	55,888	1.10	3.8	1.75	16
DuPont (EI) Nem	123	387	9,593	5.50	4.5	9.30	13
Caterpillar Tractor	54¾	396	37,659	1.50	2.7	4.45	12
Procter & Gamble	76¼	401	21,687	2.60	3.4	5.38	14
Continental Oil.........	34¾	402	34,889	1.20	3.5	4.38	7
Standard Oil of Cal	39½	421	33,976	2.20	5.6	5.18	7
Schlumberger, Ltd	59⅛	360	26,964	0.80	1.4	3.41	17
Warner-Lambert........	26	406	22,694	1.00	3.8	2.01	12
Texas Utilities.........	19⅞	382	29,430	1.40	7.0	2.29	8
Philip Morris..........	53¼	369	25,737	1.30	2.4	4.47	11
Johnson & Johnson.....	66½	344	16,177	1.10	1.7	3.53	18
Pfizer, Inc............	28⅛	386	21,714	0.96	3.4	2.28	12
Int'l Paper	56	351	20,302	2.00	3.6	5.60	10
Halliburton Co.........	55⅝	345	23,372	1.24	2.2	5.22	10
Coca-Cola Co	76½	345	16,415	3.08	4.0	4.76	16
Goodyear Tire & Rub	19¾	345	25,480	1.10	5.6	1.69	11
Monsanto Co	74⅝	333	12,017	2.80	3.8	10.05	7
Avon Products.........	47	320	21,229	2.00	4.3	2.90	16
Tenneco, Inc..........	32¼	325	27,646	1.88	5.8	4.33	7

Alcan Aluminum Ltd.	26½	265	8,602	0.80	3.0	1.14	23
Lilly (ELI) & Co.	42⅝	298	24,109	1.42	3.3	2.90	14
Weyerhaeuser Co.	38¾	321	3,331	0.80	2.1	2.32	16
McDonald's Corp.	40½	285	18,646	0.10	0.2	2.72	14
Int'l Tel & Tel.	31¾	331	25,940	1.76	5.5	3.95	8
Schering-Plough.	36⅝	305	23,955	1.00	2.7	2.91	12
Penney (J.C.)	39¼	324	28,090	1.48	3.8	3.57	10
Commonw'l Edis	29⅜	296	13,350	2.40	8.2	3.28	8
Bristol-Myers.	62⅝	294	11,013	2.20	3.5	4.90	12
Reynolds (R.J.) Ind	63⅞	293	14,260	3.28	5.1	7.48	8
Florida Pwr & Light.	25	282	16,630	1.56	6.2	2.23	11
Federated Dept Stor.	39¼	281	18,310	1.46	3.7	3.50	11
Morgan (J.P.) & Co.	50¼	272	14,133	2.00	4.0	5.04	9
U.S. Steel.	45⅝	274	15,937	2.20	4.8	5.03	9
Southern Co	16½	288	12,061	1.46	8.8	1.77	9
Texas Instruments	82⅝	242	11,276	1.32	1.6	4.25	19
Deere & Co.	30½	263	24,241	1.10	3.6	3.94	7
Sperry Rand	35⅜	239	13,755	0.92	2.6	4.32	8
RCA Corp.	28¼	269	13,399	1.20	4.2	2.30	12
Southern Cal Edison.	23⅜	257	15,231	2.00	8.6	3.70	6
Kerr-McGee.	62⅝	239	8,225	1.25	2.0	5.19	12
Middle South Util	16	259	18,116	1.38	8.6	1.72	9
BankAmerica Corp	25⅛	257	35,801	0.80	3.2	2.40	10
CBS Inc	58½	227	9,161	2.00	3.4	5.75	10
Westinghouse Elec	18¾	242	17,323	0.97	5.2	2.54	7
Digital Equipment.	41	211	20,566	—	—	2.22	18
Emerson Electric	33⅝	249	19,789	1.00	3.0	2.13	15
Central & South West . . .	16	261	23,122	1.26	7.9	1.75	9
General Foods	31½	260	12,019	1.64	5.2	3.45	9
Georgia-Pacific	32⅜	250	26,005	0.80	2.5	2.17	14
Gillette Co	27¼	218	9,006	1.50	5.5	2.58	10
Colgate-Palmolive.	24¾	263	19,798	0.88	3.6	1.95	12
Honeywell, Inc	46¾	204	6,307	1.60	3.4	4.53	10

Prices are high and low ranges for all of 1977 to cutoff date of table.

Yields and Indicated Rate are based on annual amount of dividends expected to be paid by the company based on most recent payment, assuming same rate will be continued over the next year.

Earnings, in general, are per share as reported by company. Net operating earnings are shown for banks: earnings before appropriation to general reserve for savings & loan associations; Foreign issues traded ADR are dollars per share, converted at prevailing exchange rate.

Per share earnings last 12 months indicates earnings through period indicated by superior number preceding figure: [1]for Jan., [2]for Feb., etc. Figure without superior number indicates fiscal year end.

Dividends—The following footnotes have been used in "Paid 1976" column:

K = Includes extra.
U = Includes extra and stock.
g = In Canadian funds, less 15% or 10% nonresidence tax re % Canadian ownership.
R = Less tax at origin.
N = Also stock.

% Payout 5-year average:

y = In certain years dividends exceeded available earnings.

Growth rate shows the compounded annual rate of per share earns for the latest 5 years.

Source: *Growth Leaders on the Big Board,* New York Stock Exchange, 1977. Reprinted by permission of the New York Stock Exchange.

As we move on, keep this idea in mind: If you stick with the lowest price/earnings ratio stocks—those providing the highest earnings yields—you'll outperform the rest of the market.

But earnings yields are only half the story. They must rest on a solid foundation. Which brings us to the second part of our formula.

CHAPTER 5

Book Value: The Best Guarantee You've Got

The hazards inherent in the purchase of common stocks can be all but eliminated if you purchase the right ones. Our formula insists that you do.

We buy only those stocks selling at a price below their book value.

Now what is book value, and how does it protect us?

Value is a realistic appraisal of what a company is worth. Appraisals vary, and particularly so as the state of the world changes, but for the moment let us think of value as what the company's assets could be sold for if its directors decided to cease operations. Suppose the company had net assets worth $10 million and 1 million shares of stock outstanding. Its book value would be $10 a share. If the company stopped earning money and went out of business you would still receive $10 for every share that you owned. If you paid $10 a share originally you haven't lost any money. If you paid less than $10 the liquidation will actually make you a profit. For example, Overseas National Airways, a charter airline company that sold as low as $2.25 a share in 1977, was liquidated in 1978 and 1979 at over $8, its current book value per share. It happens all the time.

Book value is, above all, a safeguard—your guarantee against catastrophic loss. If you buy a stock that's selling below its book value, and the company continues to earn money, your investment is secure. There are, of course, some risks associated with the book value of a company. These risks are very similar to the risks that face you and your net worth. For instance, the company's book value would decline if the company began to lose money. The book value is also subject to erosion if for some reason the value of its assets should decline.

But if you buy a stock selling far above its book value, or hold a stock after it's risen above that value, look out.

Back in my high-flying, high-rolling, pre-Equity Funding days, I became enchanted with a stock called Life Sciences. I had heard about the stock from another analyst who had a friend in the company. Life Sciences, he'd been informed, was on the verge of nothing less than the development of a cure for cancer. It was a classic case of a little knowledge being a dangerous thing. I bought a lot of shares at $14 a share. I knew it was a risky investment because the company's finances were in terrible shape; not only were there no earnings to speak of, there was little if any book value. Sure enough, when the cure didn't materialize, the down-side risk turned out to be 99 percent. The stock plummeted below $1 a share, and it's still selling there today. I lost $125,000.

Then there was the insurance stock that I bought because I thought the management was so good. It turned out that the management was bad, the accounting was sloppy, and the sales force ineffectual, but for awhile the company fooled a lot of people. When I bought my shares, they were selling just under their book value, but in short order the demand of investors seduced by the company's hype pushed up the price of the stock until it was selling at five times what I had paid for it—and far above its book value. Instead of taking my profits I stuck with the stock and eventually lost everything. Had I followed the principles I use today, I would have gotten out when the price of the stock went way above its book value.

Since Equity Funding I have tried religiously to follow the principle of buying a stock that sells below its book value, and there are times when I am very happy that I did, as witness the following example.

When you manufacture something you carry it on your books at its cost to you; if you can't sell it at that cost you're in trouble. That shouldn't happen to a good company, but occasionally it does. Regency Electronics was a stock in which I had made a lot of money in the early 1970s, in a somewhat bungled manner that I'll detail further on. The company made the mistake of manufacturing $5 million worth of citizens' band radios just as the market for these dried up. It unloaded the radios for $1 million—which meant an immediate reduction of its book value by $4 million. The stock, which had been selling in the high $20s, went down to $6 a share. But by then I was on the sidelines because Regency had gone so far above its book value.

There are exceptions to the rule that you sell when a stock goes above its book value, as we'll see in Chapter 8, but for the moment let's just get it fixed in our minds that book value can tell us when to sell as well as it can tell us when to buy.

Why Buy Overvalued Stocks When Undervalued Ones Are for Sale?

When we shop for a house or a car or appliances, or even clothing or food, we seldom make a purchase without first ascertaining that we're getting a good price. Not only do we satisfy ourselves that the article we're buying is the kind we want, we make sure that we're getting it as inexpensively as we can.

Please tell me why, when it comes to the purchase of securities valued in the tens and even hundreds of thousands of dollars, investors rarely do that.

A broker calls his client and says, "I think you ought to buy 500 shares of Zippity Doo Da. We think the stock can double." The investor might ask what the company does, and what it's selling for. He might even even ask about the earnings. But he never—or almost never—asks the most vital question of all: *"What is the company worth?"*

Can you imagine buying a house in that way? Never. You'd find out what other houses like it and in the same neighborhood were selling for. You'd find out what it would cost to replace the house. You'd ascertain the value of the land or of vacant lots in the neighborhood. Gradually, you'd arrive at a feeling for the market value of the house. Finally, you'd make an offer.

The cavalier attitude investors exhibit when buying stocks goes back to the follow-the-trend theory of the market. What does value matter so long as someone behind you is willing to pay more for the stock than you did? Consider the Great Tulip Craze in Holland a few centuries back, when investors bid up the prices of the most perfect bulbs to a point where each one was worth a fortune. Then one day a sailor who had just come into port picked up a bulb off a grocery counter and, thinking it was an onion, ate it. The market for tulip bulbs collapsed.

Value matters. It's not the whole story, but if it isn't part of the story there is no story, as far as I'm concerned.

When so many stocks are undervalued in today's market, why play around with stocks that are overvalued? It makes no sense at all.

It's a lot easier these days to find stocks selling below their book value than it is to find houses selling below the market price. In the last several years, the prices of stocks in relation to their book value were lower than at any time since World War II. At the end of 1977, the book value of the Dow Jones Industrial Index was $842; the Index itself stood at 818. Near the end of 1978, the book value of the Index had increased to nearly 900, while the Index itself was struggling to stay above 800.

Why Price and Value Must Eventually Coincide

Price and value don't always match. There are periods when stocks are overvalued, and periods when they're undervalued. We're delighted when stocks we've bought when they were undervalued become overvalued; we just don't want to be involved in the reverse situation.

Historically, price and value do tend to move inexorably toward a meeting ground. It's as inevitable that you'll profit from the purchase of an undervalued stock as it is that you'll lose money from buying one that's overvalued, assuming in the case of the undervalued stock that it meets our other criteria.

If a company makes money, its book value is going to increase. If the company is one that pays dividends, it might increase its dividend rate but it probably won't pay out all of its earnings because it will want some of that money for expansion. Whatever it holds back is the amount by which its book value increases. If it earns $1 a share but distributes only 40 cents a share in dividends, its book value rises by 60 cents a share.

In 1977, the 50 leading stocks that make up the Dow Jones Industrial Average distributed dividends equal to 4.5 percent of their book value. They retained earnings equal to 5.5 percent of their book value. As a consequence, the book value of these stocks increased by 5.5 percent, in this case, 44 points, from 798 to 842.

As the book value of a company increases year after year, it's inconceivable that the price of its stock won't also rise

BOOK VALUES VS.

The key is the bottom line. It shows all the years
and the few recent years in

As of 12-31	1957	1958	1959	1960	1961	1962	1963	1964
Allied Chem	42.23	42.72	44.70	23.19	23.84	22.99	24.26	23.69
Alum Co Am	....	....	35.53	36.15	36.61	38.35	39.76	37.37
Amer Brands	63.26	66.81	71.05	37.36	39.59	20.42	21.49	22.53
Amer Can	28.69	29.85	30.61	30.97	31.89	34.09	35.38	31.90
Amer Smelt	51.92	52.95	....	....	....	....	....	....
Amer Tel	153.73	157.70	54.48	56.50	59.82	62.99	65.75	35.35
Anaconda Co	....	....	85.85	87.68	89.11	91.87	94.96	97.54
Beth Steel	34.10	34.65	34.72	35.87	36.19	34.94	36.53	35.31
Chrysler	83.92	79.22	77.56	79.18	79.04	87.64	24.01	27.17
Corn Prod	19.71	18.66	....	....	....	....	....	....
du Pont	45.41	48.49	51.15	54.43	58.09	51.06	47.60	39.66
Eastman K.	30.28	32.56	17.70	18.90	20.03	21.22	22.27	22.86
Esmark	....	....	65.33	66.37	64.38	66.03	67.27	68.26
Exxon	28.63	30.35	31.17	31.78	33.00	35.39	37.19	39.02
Gen'l Elec	14.09	15.30	16.84	17.34	18.30	19.65	20.55	21.26
Gen'l Foods	23.42	25.59	27.77	15.08	16.17	17.52	18.87	20.34
Gen'l Motors	16.22	16.54	17.73	19.20	19.89	21.81	23.53	25.22
Goodyear	45.78	47.24	16.94	17.84	18.84	20.10	21.70	23.32
Inco Ltd	33.22	33.88	37.64	20.46	22.07	23.45	24.89	24.98
Int Harvester	49.86	50.54	54.34	67.39	68.10	68.98	70.52	72.51
Int'l Paper	56.07	57.40	59.58	20.23	20.50	20.64	20.90	21.39
John-Man	29.40	29.68	31.37	32.52	33.30	33.71	34.96	36.32
Minn Min Mfg	....	....	....	....	....	....	....	....
Nat'l Dist	24.11	24.92	....	....	....	....	....	....
Nat'l Steel	58.97	60.74	....	....	....	....	....	....
Owens Ill.	....	....	32.28	33.91	35.82	37.83	40.94	43.81
Proc & Gam.	23.20	24.68	27.23	29.77	16.27	17.56	18.97	20.92
Sears Roe	16.11	17.07	18.33	19.51	20.95	22.42	24.39	26.46
Std of Calif	29.73	31.83	33.91	36.14	35.29	36.23	38.76	39.53
Texaco	36.46	39.11	41.59	44.32	24.09	25.53	27.59	28.17
Union Carb	27.93	28.62	30.84	32.46	33.64	35.73	37.60	40.91
U S Steel	51.04	53.17	54.41	56.56	56.60	56.66	57.95	60.09
United Tech	34.35	38.14	39.93	39.83	39.19	40.11	41.51	43.57
Westinghouse El	44.80	47.18	50.01	26.09	25.70	25.70	25.37	25.41
Woolworth	74.87	88.22	105.81	126.14	115.86	105.81	136.41	36.61
Total	1,271.51	1,323.81	1,296.40	1,213.17	1,192.17	1,198.10	1,201.88	1,091.48
DJ Indus-Divisor	4.257	4.257	3.824	3.28	3.09	2.988	2.822	2.615
DJI Book Value	298.69	310.97	339.02	369.87	385.82	400.97	425.90	417.39
Next yr DJI mkt low	436.89	574.46	566.05	610.25	535.76	646.79	766.08	840.59
Ratio Mkt to Bk Value	146	185	167	165	139	161	180	201

p-Preliminary

DOW JONES INDUSTRIAL AVERAGE

in which these stocks have sold above their book value,
which they have sold below.

1965	1966	1967	1968	1969	1970	1971	1972	1973	1974	1975	1976
24.48	25.20	25.18	24.10	24.63	26.02	26.85	28.00	30.23	34.17	35.11	37.52
39.39	42.75	45.84	48.70	52.48	55.01	55.48	58.22	40.60	44.37	45.30	47.82
22.85	23.88	23.72	23.25	24.62	13.46	14.79	16.81	18.37	19.70	21.99	24.25
33.51	35.50	35.93	37.93	39.03	40.01	40.51	35.31	36.69	34.47	41.93	43.35
......	......	......	......	......	......	......	......	......	......	......	......
37.06	38.84	40.57	42.17	43.88	45.52	47.52	50.31	55.08	59.74	64.46	69.81
101.25	108.27	49.12	50.94	53.27		54.28	37.51	44.04	47.49	57.37	54.82
37.13	39.05	40.39	42.83	44.62	44.61	46.22	48.05	51.59	57.03	59.82	61.66
33.78	36.02	37.89	42.81	42.72	42.40	43.82	46.87	49.74	44.47	39.45	46.10
......	......	......	......	......	......	......	......	......	......	......	......
42.43	45.50	47.77	51.75	51.00	55.22	61.34	64.67	71.48	74.52	76.35	81.90
12.71	14.78	20.18	11.28	12.52	13.70	14.97	16.95	19.19	21.12	22.87	24.84
68.56	67.17	33.01	25.93	26.54	26.74	28.75	32.57	35.66	40.75	34.64	33.43
40.54	41.92	44.15	45.83	46.93	48.95	52.03	55.07	61.63	70.71	76.10	41.22
23.49	24.59	26.28	28.16	28.70	29.83	16.27	17.91	18.51	20.28	21.92	23.05
21.99	23.61	24.07	26.57	26.21	14.13	14.07	14.78	15.81	17.09	18.95	21.18
27.47	29.27	31.17	32.91	34.64	33.39	36.75	39.85	43.00	43.01	45.15	49.81
25.20	27.28	29.51	32.26	17.52	18.49	20.01	21.80	23.32	24.37	25.35	25.94
26.87	28.11	30.16	12.74	13.08	14.53	14.45	14.96	16.84	18.72	19.34	20.42
38.16	38.71	40.21	41.14	41.70	42.06	42.10	43.87	46.21	49.08	50.14	53.94
22.16	23.34	24.02	23.79	24.29	23.68	22.97	23.65	25.47	30.84	32.70	37.88
38.29	40.44	42.16	43.93	23.28	24.51	24.87	25.97	27.58	30.04	30.81	31.37
......	......	......	......	......	......	......	......	......	......	......	17.73
......	......	......	......	......	......	......	......	......	......	......	......
......	......	......	......	......	......	......	......	......	......	......	......
25.64	27.85	29.46	30.82	33.09	34.47	36.78	39.58	46.81	50.99	55.19	65.66
20.69	21.36	22.91	25.26	28.18	15.41	16.97	18.89	21.20	23.33	25.35	28.10
14.27	16.14	19.21	20.66	22.29	23.97	26.07	28.76	31.75	33.21	33.44	37.22
42.90	44.11	49.27	52.10	52.20	54.76	57.99	61.54	34.19	37.98	38.18	41.20
30.33	32.97	36.53	39.77	21.64	23.06	24.78	26.38	29.39	33.13	31.96	33.16
22.29	24.27	27.31	27.91	29.10	29.74	30.33	31.89	34.67	41.35	45.51	50.77
62.94	61.32	62.59	63.62	66.47	65.54	66.60	67.89	72.21	82.23	89.39	62.39
33.31	35.89	39.23	42.91	45.25	47.00	42.53	44.75	47.93	18.78	54.51	31.29
26.69	27.77	29.02	31.05	32.96	33.68	19.20	20.60	21.33	20.83	21.88	23.55
21.22	22.53	23.81	24.78	24.18	25.47	26.71	27.87	29.02	29.94	31.76	33.93
1,017.60	1,068.44	1,030.67	1,047.90	1,027.02	1,019.64	1,009.24	1,067.81	1,102.99	1,193.62	1,244.37	1,200.49
2.245	2.245	2.163	2,011	1.894	1.779	1.661	1.661	1.598	1.598	1.588	1.504
453.27	475.92	476.50	521.08	542.25	573.15	607.61	642.87	690.23	746.95	783.61	798.20
744.32	786.41	825.13	769.93	631.16	797.97	889.15	788.31	577.60	632.04	858.71	800.85
164	165	173	148	116	139	146	123	84	85	110	100

eventually. As its value increases, investors are willing to pay more for the stock—or, to be a little more specific, as those investors who do pay attention to value begin to take larger positions in a stock whose value is increasing, their activity comes to the attention of the follow-the-trend investors, who then buy the stock, forcing the price up still further.

But let's consider the extremely unlikely prospect that investors won't acknowledge the increase in a company's value by increasing their patronage. Once again we're in a circumstance where the company, itself, will buy back its own stock. And let's assume that you own one share of stock in this company, which we'll call Solid Rock Insurance.

The company's doing great but the market's in the doldrums so, one day, Solid Rock is selling at 50 percent of its book value. "This is ridiculous," says the president of Solid Rock. "Let's go into the market and buy our own shares back. They're selling for half of what they're worth." Every share of its own stock that Solid Rock manages to buy at 50 percent below its book value gives the company a 100 percent return; the shares—worth, let's say, $10 apiece—are bought for $5 apiece. Each share that's bought by the company for $5 reduces a $10 claim against the company, a 100 percent profit on which there is no tax. Each share purchased reduces the number of people who will share the pie by that much more, so the company keeps buying. If Solid Rock's net worth were $10 million, the market value of its stock were $5 million, and the company was able to buy back all $5 million worth of its stock at 50 percent of its book value, that would eliminate all of the shares. It's inconceivable that they could buy back all of those shares at that price, but, just for the hell of it, let's suppose they could.

All but one. Yours. Your one remaining share would be worth $5 million.

A company is owned by its shareholders. If every one of the shareholders but you was foolish enough to sell his shares for $5 apiece, you'd be the sole owner of Solid Rock.

There are companies that don't have the cash to buy back their own stock when it is selling below book value. They've got earnings problems. In that case, you don't have the kind of protection you had in the case of Solid Rock; all you have is protection in the event of liquidation. But if a company has earnings problems and you were following our criteria you wouldn't be in the stock to begin with.

Betting on Book Value

We're in a period when the prices of some stocks are crazy in relation to their value. Bad specific news in a market with a general case of the jitters can knock prices down precipitously. Just as they do when buying a stock, investors fail to ask a key question when they sell it: "What's the company worth?"

Hanover Insurance Company had a very bad year in 1975, as did insurance companies generally. The company's earnings were down, and so was its book value. Then Hanover cut its dividend sharply. The stock, which had sold as high as $40 a share, plunged all the way to $6 a share—diving right past its book value of $22 a share.

So, at $6 a share, Hanover was selling for 30 percent of its value, an almost unheard-of proposition. The selling pressure was coming from a lot of people who had bought the stock for its dividend: they had a great psychological attachment to dividends; to them, a stock without a dividend was a stock without value. Had they only asked themselves what the company was worth, they might not have lost their capital.

Value-minded investors who knew how ridiculously cheap Hanover was at $6 a share bought all they could get. Within a few years, the stock was selling for $30 a share—still, incidentally, under its book value, which had risen in the interim to $37 a share.

When a stock sells below its book value, it means that you're paying less for it than the original investor paid. You're doing better than he did when he started the company.

The first question that comes to your mind is, "If the stock's selling so cheaply, doesn't that mean that the company's doing poorly and the original investor has lost money?"

Possibly, but not probably. In most cases, the original investor probably did very well. But then the company got bigger and at some point the price of its securities went down below their value. That could indicate trouble, but the fact is that most companies selling below book today are doing so because of market conditions, other illogical factors, or both.

A few years ago, Consolidated Edison, the big New York City utility, failed to get the rate increase it felt it needed to make decent money. The company cut its dividend in half. Result? Another dramatic plunge to a level far below book value. Con Ed, which sold as low as $6 a share, rose steadily from that point to $25 a share.

Is book value always believable? No. When the price of a stock drops far below its book value, it immediately casts suspicion on that value. At that point, you should determine whether the company is continuing to make sales and develop earnings. If it is, your investment should be okay.

Most often, a great discrepancy between price and book value is simply a consequence of selling by panicky investors who don't know what they're doing. There was no way that Con Ed was going to go bankrupt, as some investors actually feared it would; eventually, the company was going to get the rate increase it needed in order to stay in business, because the city couldn't do without it.

The book values of companies are generally listed in their annual reports. You can also find corporate book values in the financial weeklies. If neither of those sources is at hand, you can ascertain the book value of a company by dividing the number of shares of its common stock outstanding into an item called "total stockholders' equity."

However you ascertain a company's book value, just be sure you do it. Don't buy a stock that's selling above its book value, no matter what anyone tells you. The stock they're touting may make money, but you'll be making money elsewhere at the same time in another, safer investment. Why take a chance when you don't need to?

CHAPTER 6
Putting It Together

A price/earnings ratio of seven to one or less.

A book value equal to or greater than the price of the stock.

If you will apply these two tests to any stock you are thinking of buying you'll be using the two best safeguards you can find.

I said in Chapter One that had the principles I now follow been adhered to by other investors, no one would have bought Equity Funding stock. Now that we understand the principles of price/earnings ratio and book value, we can demonstrate why.

In the unpublished last annual report of Equity Funding, it alleged earnings for 1972 of $2.81 a share. The stock was selling at $28 a share just before the news broke—exactly ten times its earnings. It had sold much, much higher in previous years, but even at that level, ten times earnings, it would not have been a buy because it was above our seven-to-one cutoff.

Our book value safeguard was even more out of balance. The per-share book value of Equity Funding stock was only $8, 28 *percent* of what the stock was selling for! Anyone following our principles would have taken one look at that discrepancy and moved on to safer investments.

Equity Funding failed both major tests as to whether a stock is a buy. It was a very "expensive" commodity.

There are, to be sure, other safeguards than price/earnings ratio and book value that have more to do with common sense than with numbers. You may already be well aware of them, but just to be on the safe side, let's get them on the record.

The first is that to be successful you have to diversify. No matter how great a company's value appears to be, something unforeseen could happen that would knock your stock in it to the floor. When you're invested in four or five companies, however, the law of averages is on your side. Something unforeseen might happen to one of your stocks, but not to all of them.

Just as diversification is insurance against loss, so does it enhance the prospect of gain. If you buy a single stock with marvelous prospects, the chances are excellent that its price will rise. But there's that small chance that it won't. If you buy three, four, or five stocks with marvelous prospects, it's almost mathematically impossible not to make money.

If you're starting with $10,000 and there's a prospect that you'll be able to add $2,000 or $3,000 a year to that, you can begin with two stocks. But if $10,000 is the maximum you'll be able to invest, then split it among at least three companies, or you may split it among as many as five.

I'd recommend that you confine your investments to no more than five companies, even if you have a lot more than $10,000 to invest. The more companies in your portfolio, the more work you have to do to follow them. You can stick with five companies until you're investing several hundred thousand dollars.

The second principle—well illustrated by Equity Funding—is that before you invest in a company you have to have some knowledge of what that company's business is and why it's been successful. All it really requires is good sense—as we'll see in the following chapters. Do the company's products make sense to you? Are they products you'd want to buy? Do they fill a need, or are they fads? Anyone who thought about it for a moment would have realized that citizens' band radios would saturate the market very quickly, and that companies with big inventories of them would take a bath. The same kind of reasoning might have been applied to Equity Funding's major product, a life insurance and mutual fund package. It made sense to Wall Street, which loves "concept" stocks, but not to the customer out shopping for insurance. He wasn't buying any.

The third principle is that to make money in common stocks you've got to give them time. You wouldn't think of buying a business and selling it six months later just because it hasn't made you rich overnight; then why should you do so with a common stock, which, after all, is a part ownership in a business?

Prior to my involvement with the Equity Funding scandal, I had never held onto a stock for more than three months. Today, there's one stock in my portfolio that's been there for five years, and I still see no reason to sell it.

Don't buy a stock that doesn't meet our criteria, but once you buy it give it a chance. Don't sell it the moment it loses momentum or drops below the price you paid for it. There's nothing that says a stock has to go up at once just because you bought it.

There are those who say that all common stock investments are speculation. I don't agree at all. It's true that to some extent you're at the mercy of other investors' emotions, but as long as your investment meets our test of value you're investing in facts, not fashions.

It takes discipline to make money in any business, but particularly in common stock investments. There are so many opportunities, and so many salesmen offering them to you, and it seems so easy to make money, lots of it, in other investments. And when some of those ways succeed you really want to kick yourself for not following them. It may be easy once or twice, but sooner or later you're going to lose.

Tips of any sort that don't follow our guidelines must be avoided, period. In order to buy stocks you'll have to deal with a stockbroker. He's going to call you every once in awhile with what sounds like a good idea. It may be a very good idea but if it doesn't meet our test, tell him you pass. His stock may double while yours goes down temporarily, but you just can't let that affect you. Reread *The Hare and The Tortoise.*

There could come a time when, using our criteria, you can't find a single investment. It's happened. I well remember writing—in May of 1969 when I opened Dirks Brothers, my first independent venture—to Warren Buffett, the man who made a fortune in American Express. Warren replied that he'd sold his holdings a few months earlier and wasn't buying any more. For years, Warren had earned an average of 30 percent a year on his money by investing in stocks with low price/earnings ratios that were also selling at or below their book value. Apparently there were no longer any stocks that met his criteria.

Buffett's timing was impeccable. In 1968, the stock market was booming; the average price/earnings ratio of the leading stocks had risen to 18.2—less than a 6 percent earnings yield. But beginning in January of 1969, the market began to fall off sharply. The Dow Jones Industrial Average, which had been over 1,000, fell to 770. In 1970, it went down to 631. In two years, the market lost 38 percent of its value.

If by some incredible circumstance the Dow Jones averages have doubled between the time this book is written and the time you are reading it, it may well be that there will be no stocks, or very few, selling at seven times their earnings. If you are unable to find stocks with that kind of price/earnings ratio you should either be sitting with cash or looking elsewhere.

When shares on the American stock market are selling at twenty times their earnings, you almost *have* to go elsewhere with your capital. That's exactly what a number of people I know did in the 1960s; they invested heavily in a company called Tokyo Marine & Fire Insurance, which was selling at only two times earnings, and made a fortune. At the end of 1978, the situation was reversed. Shares on the American stock market were at a lower average price/earnings ratio than shares on almost any other market—which accounts for the flood of foreign capital into American investments.

Winning

So far we've emphasized how to use our two major investment principles to avoid loss, which is proper, because the first rule of any investment program is to conserve your capital. But now let's move to the profit side of the ledger and show you, first, how Wall Street's best investors use these very principles to make big money, and then how you can do the same.

Any sophisticated investor reading this book will recognize the two basic principles in my investment formula as having originated with Benjamin Graham. Graham, senior author of the influential *Security Analysis*, the bible for stock market analysts, was the father of the value theory. Just before his death in 1976, he had completed research showing that anyone employing even a few of his investing guidelines from 1925 to 1975 would have beaten the Dow Jones averages by two to one. But Graham's ideas were, in my opinion, too complex for the average investor, and also too unwieldy. What I've done with his ideas is to simplify them to the point that the nonprofessional can do the job himself without having to analyze balance sheets and income statements. I've also added the "earnings yield" theory, which Graham considered a more scientific and logical expression than the P-E Ratio, and yet, inexplicably, did not develop in his writings. But anyone who reads investment advice with skepticism—a healthy attitude—can be comforted by the knowledge that my own principles have splendid ancestors.

Graham's theories gained great popularity in the 1950s and 1960s, and then suddenly became unfashionable for a simple reason. As prices rose, fewer and fewer securities qualified for buys under his formula. There came a point when his theory dictated that you be out of the market altogether; there just weren't any stocks selling at seven times earnings or less that also met Graham's other criteria. That made no sense to the money managers and brokers; if they didn't buy securities they didn't eat. So they kept on buying, possibly with your money.

But Graham retained a number of followers who adapted his theories—some of them the men I most admire on Wall Street. At the top of this list is John Templeton, whose Templeton Growth Fund gained 508 percent in the 10 year period ended December 31, 1977, a period in which the Dow Jones Average gained only 31 percent. To give you an even better idea of his accomplishment, the next best mutual fund performer gained only 203 per cent in the same period. Had you invested $10,000 in Templeton's fund on January 1, 1964, paid the acquisition charge of 7.75 percent, and reinvested all of your dividends, your shares by mid-1977 would have been worth $85,500. Even bad years have been relatively good ones for Templeton; in 1969, a year in which the Dow Jones Average dropped 15 percent, his fund was up 31 percent.

Templeton is the man who in 1939 called his broker and gave him one of the most oddball orders in the history of Wall Street. He told him to buy $100 worth of every stock on both major exchanges that was selling for no more than $1, including the stocks of bankrupt companies. Of the 104 companies that fitted the bill, 34 were bankrupt. Templeton's cost was $10,000. He held the stocks an average of four years, and realized $40,000.

His philosophy, as quoted by John Train, is music to my ears: "Search among many markets for the companies selling for the smallest fraction of their true worth. The best bargains will be in stocks that are completely neglected, that other investors are not even studying." The time the price is right "almost inevitably is when the company is in utter disfavor with the investing public. . . . There's no point in looking at a situation in the same way as everybody else—that is, with the same standards or preconceptions. You already know that the others don't like what they see, or at least have agreed on its price tag in terms of their understanding of it."

Another investor I admire enormously is Palmer Weber.

Weber was a young, 1930s radical with a Ph.D. in philosophy who switched to a career in investments in 1948. The manner in which he went about it is a lesson to us all. Weber set out on a prolonged trip around the United States, visiting corporation after corporation, meeting and talking to their managements. In many cases, this was the first time that anyone from Wall Street had ever turned up on these companies' doorsteps. One of Weber's finds was an oil and gas company in Texas. Its stock was selling at $5 a share. Weber eventually bought thousands of shares for his clients, and the stock got as high as $25 a share.

Not that it was easy for Weber to persuade his customers

to buy shares in any of the undervalued companies he had uncovered in his research. When Weber first returned to New York, he couldn't make a single sale of those issues. Six months passed. One evening he went to a client's home and argued through dinner as to why his host should buy some shares in one of these companies. The client refused. Later, the client's cook approached him. "I listened to you during dinner," she said. "Here's a thousand dollars. Invest it for me." Today, the cook's account is worth $30,000.

There are hundreds of sound, publicly-owned yet unknown companies in the United States just waiting for some Palmer Weber to come knocking on their doors, companies selling at five, four, even three times their earnings, with book values well above the price of their stocks. As one indication of how ridiculously low some stocks are selling in relation to their value, I know of one situation in which the company has decided, to hell with it, if nobody wants our stock we'll buy it back ourselves. I learned about it from the president of the company, whom I met in 1978.

"Is it a public company?" I asked him.

"Yeah, but don't tell anybody," he replied.

"Why not?"

"Because I'm buying back all the stock I can find—and at an extremely low price. I'd like to own it all."

Instead of going public, these companies are going private, and will, unless someone finds them.

You, the Expert

Don't be misled or put off by all the mumbo-jumbo that goes along with the buying and selling of common stocks. It's really very simple. If you'll do the work we're outlining here you'll know just as much about your chosen companies as the most overblown analyst on Wall Street. In fact, you'll probably know more. The realities being what they are, it's not inconceivable that you, a nonprofessional, can become *the* expert on a company because so many companies are followed by virtually no one.

Of the 5,000 actively-traded companies, there aren't more than a few hundred that you couldn't become an expert on just by being diligent. The question is, which ones?

Your best clues may be right in front of you.

The first stock Warren Buffett ever bought was a utility in his local area. The company was selling way below its book value and had excellent earnings. He bought all the stock he could find and made his first big money. The company's stock wasn't even quoted at the time.

Buffett, who started out with almost no money, today manages investment companies worth several hundred million dollars. In little more than 20 years, he has amassed a personal fortune of many millions of dollars. Needless to say, he is also at the top of the list of investors I most admire.

All that's required at the outset is an alertness to opportunity. Suppose you go to your dentist's office and discover that he's remodeled since your last visit. He's got some jet-age equipment that works at such high speeds it eliminates much of the pain. Find out who made the equipment. The company may have already been discovered, but you never know. Remember that new little company, Dynatech, manufacturing that marvelous gynecological instrument.

Opportunities go begging for want of someone to look into them—which brings us to that story I promised earlier of the bungled investment.

One day I received a call from a dealer in Indianapolis. "You ought to buy Regency Electronics," he said.

"What's it selling for?"

"It's a half, three-quarters," he answered, meaning fifty cents bid, seventy-five cents asked.

"Look", I said, "I'll pay five-eighths." He didn't take my offer, and I thought no more about it for a few days. But then it began to disturb me. The situation had sounded good. So I asked a colleague of mine if he could go out to Indianapolis to look the company over. He told me he was too busy.

The next thing we knew, the stock was selling at $2 a share, then $3, $4, $5, and $6 a share, up ten times in a year. Another dealer called and said, "You *really* ought to look into this thing. The company's going to earn $2 a share."

In those days, that was a tremendous bargain, so we finally did look into the stock and began to recommend it at $8 a share. Eventually it went to $20, split two for one and went to $40. In two years' time, the stock went from fifty cents to $80 a share. We grossed half a million dollars trading in the stock, but we really missed the big play. Our money multiplied only ten times. Had we responded to the first call, it would have multiplied a hundredfold.

Low price/earnings ratios may be a consequence of nothing more than a lack of knowledge, attention, or interest on the part of the investing public. This may be because the company is new. Or possibly because it's in a sector of the market that investors shy away from on the assumption that it's too difficult to understand. Financial companies are a great example. Banks, saving and loan companies, and insurance companies seem to predominate on any list of low price/ earnings ratio stocks. Only a relatively few specialists follow these companies and because of that their stocks tend to be undervalued.

Shortly after I joined the brokerage firm of John Muir & Company I received a call from a big mutual fund. Its representative told me that the fund was holding 150,000 shares of a company called RLI Corporation; he wondered if I might like to buy the shares. RLI's business was an unusual one; it insured contact lenses. As nearly as I could determine at the time, it had no competition. Its growth rate was excellent. So, on the surface, RLI seemed like a good prospect. But I wouldn't have touched the shares if they hadn't met our criteria. They did. The stock was selling at only five times its earnings and below its book value. I bought the shares for $750,000. Two years later they were worth $1,875,000. One client alone, who had bought 45,000 shares, made a profit of $337,500.

Here was a classic case of how money can be made in the shares of a sound but unknown company. Almost no one had heard of RLI, although it had been public for several years. No one had written a report on the company since its earliest days when, shortly after its stock went public, it had enjoyed a brief but unrealistic rise in price to 20 times earnings. As the price fell, many stockholders sold out, and the company was soon forgotten. When I learned about RLI only three brokers were making a market in its stock.

For every new company that is undiscovered there is at least one old one that the market has discarded.

Consider Mission Insurance. This was no unlisted stock. It was traded on the New York Stock Exchange. Its shares at one time had been widely held by institutions. One year it was even named the favorite stock of insurance analysts. And then, suddenly, everyone lost interest in Mission Insurance stock for no apparent reason. There were a few dips in earnings, but nothing to explain what happened, which was that the stock of Mission Insurance, which had been selling at $40 a share, dropped all the way to $8. When we found the company, it was earning $4 a share, and its price had risen to $17 a share, a little better than four times earnings, for an earnings yield of 25 percent. It was also selling a little below its book value.

We grabbed it. Within a year, earnings had jumped to $7 a share, and the stock was selling for $42.

Once in a while, we get a case in which a highly visible company shows the characteristics of a good investment and yet doesn't rise in price. Consider Ford Motor Company, which was selling in the fall of 1978 at 60 percent of its book value and at a price/earnings ratio of three-and-a-half to one. More than that, it was yielding 7.7 percent as a dividend. The company meets our standards and yet it may not be a buy precisely because it is so well known. The same pressures that make it difficult to buy Blue Chips stocks at good prices makes it difficult for them to respond when they ought to: Too many people are interpreting general information in the same way. Investors worried about an oil embargo or competition from Japan put such selling pressure on the company that it can't rise to its legitimate value.

All the more reason why you should look for undiscovered stocks.

Sweetening the Pot

Every successful investor I've mentioned to this point shares with me the conviction that an investment must pass two basic tests before it can be considered: Is the stock selling at seven times earnings or less, and is it selling below its book value? Every example I've used has met these two conditions.

To these two conditions we're now going to add a third: *growth rate.* Is the company making more money than it made the year before, and the year before that, and so on? There are market theorists who insist that before they'll buy a stock it must show a consistent growth pattern in addition to other requirements.

As should be evident by my remarks in chapter 2, I'm not a stickler on this point. What troubles me is the word "consistent." Nothing is ever consistent, certainly not in business. To make growth rate the basis of decisions is to play a long-term game with short-term rules.

Certainly it's comforting to know that a company is growing at a healthy rate each year. Certainly it's a good idea to examine that growth rate before you get involved. But if earnings are healthy to begin with in relation to price, I'm not going to kick a stock out of my portfolio just because a company has a dip in its growth rate from one quarter to the next, or even from one year to the next. I don't always make more money each quarter or year than I did the previous quarter or year. But there are usually valid reasons why I don't—and I certainly don't give up on myself as a consequence. I'm much more interested in my prospects for next year, and the year after, and five years hence. If those prospects are solid, I'm in great shape. Why shouldn't that standard apply to an investment? So others will bail out and thereby lower the price of the stock; if you know the future is exciting, buy more stock.

Having all three conditions fulfilled would be the best of all possible worlds. But it's hard to come by. For example, there were more than 400 candidates for investment based on the criteria of price/earnings ratio and book value when we took a count in October 1978. But there were only 45 companies that fulfilled the growth rate requirement as well.

Would these 45 have automatically been better investments than any of the others? Perhaps, but not necessarily. A stock selling at three times its earnings, with no significant increase in its growth rate could be a better buy than one selling at six times earnings that has a prettier growth chart.

Growth, by all means. But it doesn't have to be all that consistent, so long as it remains respectable.

Dividends: They're Nice, But Do We Want Them?

Here is another criterion with stellar advocates. They won't touch a stock unless its dividend is a certain percentage of its price. Once again, I'm not nearly so choosy. I like dividends, but only to a point.

The dividend yield of a stock is normally a percentage of the earnings yield. It reflects how much of its earnings the company is going to pay out immediately in cash, as opposed to what it's going to retain and reinvest in the company's future.

When you have an earnings yield of 20 percent per share of a stock, the chances are that at some time in the near future the dividend yield on that stock will rise to 10 percent, or half the earnings yield. If the company's growth slows and it doesn't have need to reinvest its earnings in order to finance expansion, the dividend yield on its stock could go all the way up to 20 percent. In other words, the company would pay out everything it's earned and you would, without question, have earned 20 percent on your money; you could count on it.

At that point I'd be getting nervous about holding the stock. Whether the money was held by the company, which increased its book value and stock price, or whether the money was paid directly in dividends wouldn't technically make any difference. Either way, you'd be earning 20 percent. The great hazard in the event of a dividend payment of that magnitude is that the next year the company might earn only 15 percent, Wall Street would interpret the news of the reduced dividend bearishly, and the price of the stock could plummet.

The best thing to be said about dividends is that a lot of people like them, which means that they'll support a stock that pays them.

But if it's long term-growth you're looking for, you really ought to cultivate those companies that retain much, even most, of their earnings for expansion.

Dividends are one subject on which I diverge from Benjamin Graham. One of his criteria was that dividend rates ought to equal two-thirds of the average Triple-A bond yield. Translation: If you could get back 8 percent on your money by investing in the Triple-A bonds offered by a company, you ought to get a dividend of at least 5.3 percent of your investment in that company's common stock. Otherwise, forget it.

To me, that's too restrictive a standard. It rules out situations that have great promise in more important respects. It puts a premium on a comparatively marginal return—on which a tax must be paid, to boot. And it emphasizes companies that, by virtue of their high dividends, would not be candidates for growth.

If a company is growing at a healthy rate in excess of the normal growth rate of the economy, it usually has to retain a large portion of its earnings in order to maintain its growth. It needs additional plants, equipment, and resources to handle an increasing amount of business. A company paying a high dividend drastically limits its ability to finance this additional capacity.

You have to decide at the outset what your interest is— income or capital growth. You can't turn $10,000 into $100,000 in nine years by investing in companies that pay big dividends. The companies providing earnings yields of 15 to 40 percent a year need most of what they make to sustain that rate of growth.

Choosing Companies That are
Responsive to Inflation

One question you ought to keep in mind as you look for companies in which you would like to invest is: Which industries are better than others in adjusting to long periods of significant inflation? Some industries can adjust their prices all but automatically, whereas this is a cumbersome process for others. We all know what a hassle it is for the steel industry to raise prices following the negotiation of new and cost-raising contracts with their unions; not only will the government react; the public, which will have to pay more for cars and appliances, will consider the price hike unnecessary. It may be, but if the companies don't get it, their profits are going to shrink—and that's important to you as an investor.

The telephone industry is even less responsive to inflation. Before it can raise its rates, it must seek and obtain approval from some government body. All utilities share this problem; while this doesn't rule them out as investments, it makes them relatively less desirable.

Service industries have no such problems. Their prices aren't regulated by anything but supply and demand. Their only concern is to remain competitive. They can raise their prices instantly; if their customers pay the increase without complaint, and don't take their business elsewhere, there are no problems. Monopolistic industries, in which franchises exist, are equally responsive to inflation. Newpaper and broadcasting are good examples.

The insurance industry is highly responsive to inflation. It is regulated to an extent, but it doesn't need to go off to the regulators every time it raises its rates. Generally, the price of insurance goes up to reflect the increased cost of settling claims or of replacing property that has been lost or damaged. An insurance company's profits will go up and down almost in proportion to the extent that the change in its rates reflects the rate of inflation.

Remember that an increase in earnings of 7 percent a year is really the minimum you should look for; just that increase is what is required to keep up with inflation. Anything above that is real growth—for you and the company.

Enjoy

The bottom line is whether an investment will make you money. But sometimes there are subjective considerations that ought to enter in. A distaste for *how* the money is made can keep you away from a bad investment.

If you feel that a company's endeavors are without any particularly redeeming social value, that might be a good reason for not investing in it—and not just for personal reasons, but for financial ones as well. The stocks of companies manufacturing citizens band radios might have done well when their product caught on, but perhaps you felt like I did and wondered what earthly use citizens band radios performed for the general public. Had you asked yourself whether you wanted to make money on citizens band radios, you would have had a connection between your moral posture and the financial impact of the product. Once those people who found pleasure in citizens band radios bought them, there were no further customers.

Investments in metals companies might not feel good to you because such companies make money on a wasting asset. They make a lot of money when the price for the ore is right, but it takes them that much closer to the inevitable day when there won't be enough ore left.

I happen to have an aversion to manufactured needs. There are so many worthy endeavours to which our resources ought to be applied, that it pains me to see them wasted to satisfy contrived demand. For moral reasons, therefore, I wouldn't want to profit from companies whose existence is predicated on changing styles. That coincides with my feeling as a businessman that fashion and apparel industries aren't good investments. If they happen to hit the right product for a year or two they can make a lot of money. But their earnings plummet when their styles lose favor.

There are plenty of ways to make money. Why not make it in a manner that makes you feel good? Why not find a company whose work you respect? A company in which you feel some pride in ownership? With which you feel a real connection? *Then* investing becomes more than a matter of pieces of paper. It becomes an affair of people.

It's that human connection that, added to the numbers, takes the guesswork out of investing.

CHAPTER 7
The Company You Keep

If a friend told you he'd found a marvelous investment opportunity and asked you to join him in the venture, you'd still want to ask him some questions, no matter how good a friend he was. What's the nature of the investment? Who's behind it? What makes it so good? What evidence has he seen that it's good? Who has he talked to? How reliable is their word? How much can you expect to make? How long will it take? What are the risks?

Common-sense questions. You could have no business background whatever and they would still come to mind. It's no different when you investigate a company whose shares you're thinking of buying.

First, of course, you have to find the company.

For the purpose of this exercise, let's assume that you have found no opportunities in your own community, and have not been told of any. You're starting from scratch. Nothing to worry about; within a day you'll have all the prospects you need.

You can begin your search in the most obvious place of all, the tables of the New York Stock Exchange. You can also search among the tables of the American Stock Exchange. My own favorites are the over-the-counter (OTC) stocks; I invest in them almost exclusively. I'll let Robert E. Dallos of the *Los Angeles Times* put that recommendation in perspective:

"There was a time not too long ago," he wrote in 1978, "when many investors would have chosen to shake hands with a grizzly bear rather than touch the over-the-counter securities market. Trading in OTC stocks—those not listed on one of the major exchanges—was too risky, they felt. The OTC market was too speculative a game. It was too shrouded in mystery. It was too vulnerable to the manipulations of an unscrupulous few.

"But now all that is changing. The OTC market suddenly is sporting a sparkling new image. More and more brokers are saying—and more and more customers are believing—that an investment in a widely traded but unlisted stock is no riskier than an investment in many listed securities.

"With this new image has come a dramatic upsurge in trading. Volume during the first nine months of this year in the 2,600 leading over-the-counter stocks—those quoted on the National Association of Securities' Dealers' computerized 'Nasdaq' system—totaled 2.1 billion shares, up 54 percent over the same period last year."

Dallos notes that mutual funds, bank trust departments, and other institutional investors have begun to put big dollars into the market they once spurned. Fund groups have even created "special situation" funds to focus on OTC stocks.

There are several major reasons for the OTC market's current popularity. The first, not surprisingly, is the profitability of many of its issues. As institutional traders became more and more disenchanted with their "nifty fifty" strategy, they began to look elsewhere for better opportunities. Inevitably, they came to respect the very situation that they had previously spurned—the undiscovered, undervalued company. All such companies start out by trading over the counter before achieving a listing on one of the big boards.

Other factors accounting for the OTC market's new respectability are: Greatly improved communications, which make it possible to keep abreast of market developments that previously required hours to learn about; a rise in the dividend rates of OTC securities; rise in the number of takeover candidates among the OTC companies, principally because OTC stocks tend to have a lower market value than listed securities; and a rise in the number of foreign investors.

For all of these reasons, you can feel that you're in good company when you look among over-the-counter securities. Most of the best investors I know focus their efforts almost exclusively on OTC stocks; one of my favorite investors, Ed Laufer, finds most of his investments by reading the annual reports of small companies traded over the counter.

Tools of the Trade

For the work you're about to do you'll need to have a few tools—selected publications, all of which are available in your public library, on newstands, or by subscription. However you choose to do it, here's a rundown on recommended publications:

The Wall Street Journal, Subscriber Service, 200 Burnett Road, Chicopee, Massachusetts 01021. Indispensable for daily business news, but not all that comprehensive with figures. It has the daily stock table as well as price/earnings ratios, but for statistical profiles on individual companies you have to look elsewhere.

Barron's. The Dow Jones Business and Financial Weekly, 200 Burnett Road, Chicopee, Massachusetts 01021. Dated every Monday, *Barron's* can actually be obtained as early as Saturday in some areas. It gives details of the latest quarterly or interim earnings and also tells you whether or not they are recurring earnings. But it doesn't show book value.

The Financial Weekly, P.O. Box 26991, Richmond, Virginia 23261. A publication widely used by professionals. *The Financial Weekly* lists earnings, price/earnings ratios, and book values.

Standard and Poor's, 345 Hudson Street, New York, New York 10014. A monthly stock guide, with a comprehensive picture of each company's market performance going back to 1960. Price/earnings ratios, but few book values.

Value Line Investment Survey, c/o Arnold Bernhard & Company, Inc, 711 Third Avenue, New York, New York 10017. This publication gives you both an analysis of stocks and an interpretation of opinion as to their future performance.

If I had to choose only one of the above, it would be *The Financial Weekly*. It doesn't have daily quotes and it doesn't give you much news, but it tells you everything else you need to know, as well as a lot that you don't need but might find interesting.

What you're after, essentially, are price/earnings ratios and a comparison of stock prices with book values.

While you'll want to follow the activity of your eventual investments on a day-to-day basis, let's use *The Financial Weekly* to identify the candidates.

The Treasure Hunt Begins

Step 1

Using the listing "Stocks by Industry Group" found in section 1 of *The Financial Weekly,* circle all the numbers in column nine, "P/E," that are seven or less. There are two figures under P/E, one current, the other a five-year average. You want the current figure.

Step 2

Under the section marked "Price," locate the column marked "To Common Equity." The figures in that column show the current price of a stock as a percentage of its book value. All numbers under 100 indicate stocks selling below book value. Circle all of those numbers under 100 that are next to a previously circled P/E ratio number.

We performed these two exercises in *The Financial Weekly* of December 4, 1978, and came up with an incredible total. Among the New York Stock Exchange, the American Stock Exchange, and the over-the-counter market, a selection of whose stocks are listed in these tables, there were 1,398 companies with P/E ratios of seven or less. Of these, 1,041 were also selling below their book values.

Step 3

Obviously, 1,041 stocks is more than we can handle, so we want to whittle the number down further before we get into details. For this reason, we use our growth criteria. In column twelve, under the heading "EPS" and subheading "5 Year Growth Rate," we find a number that gives us the company's compounded rate of growth during this period.

STOCKS BY INDUSTRY GROUP

Using this table from the *Financial Weekly* of the *Aerospace Industry*, we performed the first three steps of the hunt (see circles). But only two candidates were left after step two and they were eliminated by step three. You will find that the number of candidates will vary widely from industry to industry.

Company and Market	Price				Price Range				P/E		E.P.S.		Financial	
		Com-mon Equity	Change		52-Week		5-Year				Latest 12 Months RPT	5-Year Growth Rate	Return on Common Equity	Divi-dend Yield
	To Close		This Week	Last 52 Weeks	High	Low	High	Low	Cur-rent	5-Year Avg				
	1	2	3	4	5	6	7	8	9	10	11	12	13	14
	$	%	%	%	$	$	$	$			$	%	%	%
011 Aerospace Industries														
Boeing Co.......... *N	71.50	220	11.1	154.2	76.00	25.00	76.00	5.81	11.2	6.5	6.36n	40	20	2.7
Curtiss-Wri .... *N	14.50	(56)	3.6	18.3	22.25	11.88	35.63	5.00	8.1	10.5	1.78s	16	7	5.5
Fairchild Ind ...... *N	27.00	144	6.9	80.0	35.50	14.25	35.50	3.75	6.6	7.9	4.09n	23	22	3.0
Gen Dynamics ...... *N	80.50	136	8.4	64.7	93.50	37.00	93.50	13.50	NC	5.4	6.27n	18	NE	.0
Grumman Corp...... *N	15.63	(62)	.7	6.0	24.88	14.75	24.88	7.28	(5.0)	5.1	3.10n	10	12	7.7
Lockheed Corp...... *N	20.38	115	5.2	27.3	37.63	12.88	37.63	2.75	6.0	3.5	3.40n	21	19	.0
McDonnel Doug..... *N	34.88	113	13.9	45.3	40.50	22.75	40.50	7.63	8.9	6.4	3.91n	4	13	1.7
Northrop Corp..... *N	35.50	158	2.0	69.0	49.88	18.75	49.88	4.69	6.6	5.8	5.39s	50	24	4.5
Rockwell Intl....... *N	34.50	(95)	4.5	17.9	38.00	28.88	38.00	18.00	(6.3)	7.4	5.45f	10	15	7.0
Thermo Electron.... 0	25.00	153	6.4	53.8	31.75	13.75	31.75	6.25	12.1	17.7	2.07q	24	13	.0
Unit Technols....... *N	38.63	124	1.6	7.7	52.50	32.25	52.50	10.38	8.3	7.7	4.64n	17	15	5.2

From December 4, 1978 issue of The M/G Financial Weekly. Reprinted by permission of Media General.

Of the stocks that qualified in Steps 1 and 2, circle those with growth rates of 15 percent or more.

Result on December 4, 1978: Four hundred eighty—the highest number, by far, that I can ever remember.

Step 4

Obviously the list is still much too unwieldy. So here you can begin to exercise some personal preferences. Are you more interested in certain industries than in others? Do you have special knowledge that puts you at an advantage? Do you have convictions that would prompt you to eliminate certain groups? As we saw in chapter 6, these convictions can be important considerations from an investment point of view. For example, I don't smoke. Neither do most of my friends—many of whom once did. I figure if so many people have stopped smoking, the trend eventually has to catch up with the tobacco industry. I wouldn't think of buying a tobacco stock.

Step 5

Theoretically, any of the remaining stocks is a candidate for investment. But we'd like to refine the list still further.

Make a comparison of all those stocks that qualify in terms of their P/E ratio, book value, earnings growth, and personal preference. Which ones have the *lowest* P/E ratios? Which are selling the *most* below book value? Which have the *highest* growth rates compounded over the last five years?

Isolate those stocks on the list that best reflect all of these excellent characteristics.

I went the long way around on this treasure hunt because I wanted to prove two points—that, first, there are more bargains available today in common stocks than ever before and, second, that even an inexperienced investor can locate them with only a few hours' work. There is a more direct route—to execute step 4 first, deciding which industry or groups of industries you want to focus on.

Using the short-cut, focusing on my specialty, the insurance industry, I still came up with 85 candidates after step 1. Step 2 narrowed the list to 55. Step 3 narrowed it still further to 37. Step 5 reduced my list to the 15 most attractive investments based on P/E ratio, book value, and growth rate that I could find on December 4, 1978.

		% of Book Value	P-E Ratio	5 Year Growth Rate
American National Financial	OTC	72	5.0	20
Avemco	ASE	72	5.4	73
Kentucky Central Life	OTC	65	4.4	17
National Liberty	OTC	66	5.5	17
Penn Life	OTC	55	4.9	25
Travelers Corp.	NYSE	72	4.2	20
American General Insurance	NYSE	61	5.0	22
Cimarron Investment	OTC	56	1.7	25
CNA Financial	NYSE	70	4.5	39
Continental Corp.	NYSE	73	4.3	24
Crum & Forster	NYSE	84	4.0	26
Financial Security Group	OTC	61	2.8	40
INA Corp.	NYSE	76	4.9	17
Kemper Corp.	OTC	80	3.5	36
Ticor	NYSE	61	5.3	23

Let us emphasize that this was the list as of December 4, 1978. It is not a list on which to base any investments today.

One caution: it takes a while to update stock tables that carry more than daily transaction information. Before buying a stock, it is imperative that you double-check the figures. A sudden, huge loss might not yet be reflected in the tables you've been using; in that case the table might show a low P/E figure and a good book value rather than a negative P/E and a severely reduced book value.

Going through this process, one of my associates found a company called Jewelcor, which sells jewelry and household items by catalogue. The stock looked beautiful on paper, with a very low price/earnings ratio and a price well below book value. But he then called the company and learned that it had lost a great deal of money in the previous quarter, which was why the stock was so cheap. That development was not reflected in the tables I was using.

The other item to which you should pay close attention is the big "X" next to earnings that you'll find in certain instances in *Barrons*. This indicates the inclusion of a "non-recurring" profit. Investments are based on the ability of profits to be sustained. If a company's good record is based on a one-time deal, that's not going to be interpreted all that bullishly by other investors.

A STOCK TABLE FROM BARRONS

Symbols to watch for: × Includes non-recurring profit, ➧ **New earnings. We have circled the symbols we are watching.**

												EARNINGS		DIVIDENDS		
52-Weeks				Sales	Yield	P-E		Week's		Net		Interim or	Year	Latest	Stk	Payment
High	Low	Stock	(div.)	100s	Pct.	Ratio	High	Low	Last	Chg.		Fiscal yr	ago	dec	of rec	date
20½	12¾	ABaker	1.20b	66	8.9	6	13½	13	13½	+ ½		Oct40wl.54	⊗2.15	q.30+S5%	9-25	10-15
53	39⅜	ABrnds	4	816	8.0	7	50¼	49¼	50	+ ⅛		Sep9m5.67	4.56	q1.00	11-10	12-1
25½	22⅛	ABrd	pf 1.70	19	7.2		24	23½	23⅝	+ ⅛		77Dec59.65	42.00	q.42½	11-10	12-1
43¼	33⅞	ABdcst	1.20	2808	3.2	8	37¾	35⅝	37¾	+2		Sep9m3.26	2.75	q.30	11-24	12-15
20½	12½	ABldM	.60	34	3.9	8	15¼	14¾	15¼	+ ⅛		July9m1.48	1.32	q.15	10-13	10-31
43⅜	34⅝	AmCan	2.70	744	7.6	6	37½	35⅜	35¾	−1⅜		Sep9m4.61	4.18	q.67½	10-20	11-25
23⅝	20¾	ACan	pf 1.75	23	8.1		21⅝	21¼	21⅝	+ ⅛	+	77Dec65.36	57.84	q.43¾	12-8	1-2
4⅞	2⅛	ACentry		358			3⅛	2⅜	3⅛	+ ¾		Sep3mD.07	D.19	Y		2-22-74
45⅛	16⅛	ACredt	1.30	149	3.2	11	42	40¾	41	− ⅞		Sep9m3.02	⊗2.75	q.32½	11-15	12-1
32⅞	22⅝	ACyan	1.50	1770	6.0	8	25½	24½	25	− ⅜		Sep9m2.34	2.15	q.37½	11-24	12-22
13¼	8	AmDistl		146			9¼	8½	9¼	+ ¼	(➧)	78SepX.04	Def	Y		1-3-75
36	22⅝	ADT	1.08	x935	4.7	9	24½	d22⅝	23	−1⅜		Sep9m1.91	1.91	q.27	12-1	12-20
11¾	6½	ADualVt		23			9¼	9	9¼	+ ¼				Y		3-31-72
14¾	14⅛	ADul	pf .84a	21	5.8		14¾	14⅜	14⅜			77Dec.94	.83	q.21	9-15	9-29
24¾	20¾	AElPw	2.18	2117	9.9	9	22⅛	21½	22⅛	+ ½		Sep12m2.41	2.46	q.54½	11-6	12-8
40⅝	29⅝	AmExp	1.60	3289	5.0	8	32¼	31⅛	31¾	+ ¼	+	Sep9m3.19	2.69	q.40	1-5	2-9
17⅛	9¼	AFamil	.60	899	6.0	5	10⅜	9¼	10	− ⅛		Sep9m1.62	1.73	q.15	11-15	12-1
9¼	4⅛	AmFnSys		285		12	8⅝	8¼	8⅝	+ ⅛		Sep9m.64	.73	Y		6-16-75
27⅛	15⅝	AFnSy	pf	z710			27	25¾	27	+1		77Dec8.42	4.66	Y		6-16-75
24⅝	19⅝	AGlBd	1.96e	256	9.5		21	20⅝	20⅝	− ⅜		78Jun1.98	1.99	.16	11-17	11-30
19	16	AGnCv	1.32	91	7.9		16⅝	16⅛	16⅝	+ ¼	+	Jun6m.60		M.11	11-30	12-15

29¾	21½	AGnIns	1	690	4.0	4	24⅞	24	24¾	+ ⅞		Sep9m5.41	4.88	q.25	11-10	12-1
36¾	27⅞	AGln	pf 1.80	168	5.8		31¼	30⅝	30⅞	+ ⅝		77Dec18.54	10.13	q.45	11-10	12-1
29½	21⅜	AGln	pf .90	2	3.8		23¾	23¾	23¾			77Dec18.54	10.13	q.22½	11-10	12-1
13	8½	AHeritLf	.40	35	4.1	7	10⅜	9⅞	9⅞	− ½		Sep9m1.12	1.03	q.10	11-6	11-17
23½	12	AmHoist	1	809	6.6	7	15½	14½	15¼	+ ⅜		Sep42w1.70	2.40	q.25	11-15	12-11
32¾	26⅛	AHome	1.40	5232	5.1	13	28½	27⅛	27½	− ⅞		Sep9m1.64	1.45	q.35	11-13	12-1
142¾	117	AHome	pf 2	2	1.6		124½	124½	124½	− ¾	+	77Dec943.30	749.47	q.50	12-13	1-1
32¾	22⅝	AmHosp	.68	3498	2.6	11	26¼	24¼	25⅞			Sep9m1.71	1.41	q.17	11-29	12-18
13⅛	4¾	AmInvst	.30	349	2.8	20	10¾	10½	10⅝			Sep9m.52	.60	q.07½	11-13	12-1
31¾	16⅝	AMI	.60b	1385	2.6	9	23⅝	21¼	23⅜	+1⅜		78Aug2.53	1.89	q.15	1-5	2-1
7⅛	3⅝	AmMotrs		1630		7	5⅜	5	5¼			78Sep.80	.10	Y		9-25-74
47½	37⅞	ANatR	3	318	7.2	7	41¾	39⅞	41¾	+1¾		Sep12m6.30	5.88	q.75	10-13	11-1
18⅞	10¼	AShip	.80a	x78	6.5	13	12½	12⅛	12⅜	+ ½		78Sep.95	1.96	.20	12-4	1-2
53⅛	32¼	AStand	2.60	909	6.2	6	42¼	41	42			Sep9m5.55	4.15	q.65	11-21	12-24
140	87	AStd	pf 4.75	9	4.3		112	110	111	+1		77Dec179.64	34.78	q1.19	11-21	12-24
9⅜	6	ASteril	.32	401	4.9	9	6¾	6¼	6½	− ⅛		Sep9m.50	.23	q.08	11-24	12-15
37⅞	28	AmStrs	2.24	48	7.3	5	31	30¾	30¾	− ⅜		Sep26w3.15	1.92	q.56	12-8	1-2
64⅝	56⅞	ATT	4.60	8193	7.5	8	61⅜	60	61⅛	+ ⅜		Aug12m7.59	6.72	q1.15	11-30	1-2
67¼	59¾	ATT	pf 4	86	6.2		65	64	65	+ ½		77Dec142.78	85.80	q1.00	12-29	2-1
50½	44½	ATT	pf 3.64	308	7.9		46⅜	45⅞	46	− ¼		77Dec142.78	85.80	q.91	12-29	2-1
51½	45½	ATT	pf 3.74	474	7.9		47⅜	47	47⅛	− ⅛		77Dec142.78	85.80	q.93½	12-29	2-1
14	10¼	AWatWk	.84	62	7.5	5	11¼	10⅝	11¼	+ ½		Sep12m2.16	2.63	q.21	11-1	11-15
20	14¾	AWat	pf 1.43	z100	9.2		15½	15½	15½	+ ¾		77Dec26.04	24.38	q.35⅞	11-15	12-1
14¾	12	AWat	pf 1.25	z250	9.6		13	12¾	13	+ ¼		77Dec47.46	44.53	q.31¼	11-15	12-1
15	12¾	AWa	5pf1.25									77Dec32.88	29.43	q.31¼	11-15	12-1
23¼	16	Ameron	1	21	5.9	6	17⅛	16¾	16⅞	− ¼		Aug9m1.65	1.39	q.25	10-25	11-15
16⅛	9½	AmesD	.40	79	3.5	5	11⅜	10⅝	11⅜	+ ¾	◐	Oct9m1.55	1.48	q.10	11-3	12-15
37¾	27¼	Ametek	1.60	214	5.5	8	29¼	27⅜	29¼	+1⅞	+	Sep9m2.87	2.54	q.45	12-11	12-22
20⅝	14½	Amfac	1	291	5.9	6	17½	16⅝	16⅞	− ⅜		Sep9mX1.92	1.51	q.25	11-22	12-15
25¼	12¼	AMIC	.20	x1960	.8	10	25¼	24¾	25⅛	+ ¼		Sep9m1.91	1.43	q.05	12-1	1-2
40	24	AMPInc	.60	1102	1.8	13	34⅛	33	33⅜	+ ⅜		Sep9m1.93	1.51	q.15	11-6	12-1

Stock Table, December 4, 1978. Reprinted by permission of Barron's.

Step 6: Checking out Your Choice

We'll assume that you've narrowed your own list to 15 to 20 companies in several fields. From here on, it's a matter of common sense. What business is the company in? Is it responsive to inflation? Does its operation include foreign subsidiaries that could be nationalized by a new leftist government? What about the industry as a whole? Is it vulnerable to political developments? Would a drastic increase in the price of oil, for example, seriously affect its earnings?

A lot of these questions have self-evident answers. Some of them could be answered by reading the company's annual report, a copy of which you can obtain by writing or calling.

An even better resource is something called a "10-K," a relatively new report required of companies by the Securities and Exchange Commission. It includes a description of the company's business, a summary of its operations, a list of its properties, a list of its parent and subsidiary companies, any legal proceedings pending against the company, increases and decreases in the company's outstanding securities, the number of shareholders, remuneration of officers, and a host of other facts.

But the approach I favor most is the most direct—either face to face or voice to voice.

The Human Connection

There are investors I admire who almost never contact the companies they invest in; they concentrate exclusively on the figures they find in the financial journals. I don't quarrel with their success, but I would never make an investment without first contacting a company's management. It's important that you do that, too. There is all the difference in the world between owning shares in a company whose management you know and owning pieces of paper whose value fluctuates with the market. When you know what you own you stay calm in periods of adversity; when you don't, you panic.

The greatest problem in getting to know a company isn't how to go about it, it's picking up that phone. No one is perfectly comfortable when he must call a stranger, but I have some thoughts and techniques for you that should make the job easier.

First of all, the person you reach is delighted to receive your call. He's paid to talk to people just like you. He needs you, and his company needs you. True, your prospective purchase of 100 shares or even 500 shares is not the turning point in the company's fortunes, but a great many small purchases like yours could have an appreciable effect.

If a company has an antagonistic attitude toward potential stockholders and is secretive and abrasive in its dealings, it is going to turn off a lot of people. Word gets around. Willy-nilly, the company loses that extra following it needs to maintain the price of its stock.

You should make your phone call with the attitude that these people need you more than you need them. You don't have to buy their stock; there are hundreds of companies to choose from. If they don't treat you kindly or give you the information you need, you not only don't have to take it, you know that they have an attitude that's not good for business.

Remember, too, that you're no neophyte. By this point you have knowledge of what makes a stock a buy—a far more sophisticated knowledge, in fact, than the average investor; more, even, than many stockbrokers.

All companies sell something. All of them have expenses. Hopefully, a certain amount of earnings remain after the expenses. That doesn't differ an iota from your private life. You sell your services. You have living expenses. You try to make more than you spend. All the jargon in business finances really reduces to very simple terms.

Now, let's make that call.

Questions and Answers

The person you want to talk to may be any one of several people. If the company's really small, you may want to talk to the president. Don't be awed by his title; he puts his pants on one leg at a time. But the president may not be the best person to talk to; there may be someone in the firm to whom calls like yours are directed, perhaps the public relations director, perhaps the director of investor relations.

When you call, tell the switchboard operator, "I'd like to

talk to someone who can tell me about your stock." Once you're connected with the right person, here's how it would go.

You: I'm an investor. I'm interested in learning about your company. First of all, I see that it's priced very low in relation to its earnings.

Spokesman: We think so too.

You: How do you account for that?

Spokesman: We've had excellent sales for the last several years, we have excellent prospects, and it's just a question of not enough people having discovered what a good job we're doing.

You: Are you doing anything to get your story told?

Spokesman: Well, quite frankly, we're a little averse to blowing our own horn, but we're happy to tell our story to anyone who's interested.

You: *Is* anyone interested?

Spokesman: Yes, as a matter of fact. We've had several recent inquiries from brokers.

You: Have you issued any statements about the company recently that would give investors an idea of what's happening?

Spokesman: We've sent out a number of press releases. Would you like a set?

You: Yes, indeed. And your latest annual report and quarterly report. Also a 10-K. And I'd be grateful if you'd put me on your mailing list.

Let's interrupt your call for a moment to interpret what you're hearing.

When you buy a stock it's in the expectation that someone will, in the future, be willing to pay more for it than you did. That requires continued good performance from the company, but also a well-modulated effort on somebody's part to make the company known.

There is something to say for a company that plays it close to the vest. If a company puts out expensive annual reports, does a great deal of self-promoting, and boasts how good it is relative to the competition, you've really got to be suspicious. Equity Funding had one of the slickest, most active promotional programs I can remember; its officials were always traveling to Wall Street to tell analysts how good the company was. When a company spends that much for promotion, the chances are that its stock is ahead of its earnings rather than behind them—which was exactly the case with Equity Funding.

Most horn-tooting companies aren't the type that sell at low P/E ratios and way below book. If they're promotion minded, inclined to overstate their case, and even to fudge their figures, they are generally succeeding in getting their stock to a level both above its book value and above seven times earnings. Which means you wouldn't be in it.

When a company doesn't want to give you information, you could say, logically, that you wouldn't want to be involved with it. On the other hand, this reticence might be a clue as to why its stock is selling so cheaply. It may be a fine company—with a policy of not talking to anyone. That, of course, can create great bargains.

But reticence should not be confused with hostility. The deciding factor ought to be the attitude with which you're received. It's one thing not to advertise and another to be forthcoming if and when you're approached. The latter case is ideal: the company is relatively unknown, but it's willing to tell you what you need to know to make an informed investment.

Just remember that while you eventually want everyone to know about a stock you own, you don't want them to know about it until you've bought it. So if you ask the company spokesman who's buying the stock or writing it up and he says, "No one," you're way ahead of Wall Street. Discovery is the key.

Now back to your call.

The most important subject to discuss is earnings, and here you may have to do a little sparring because the company spokesman is operating under certain restrictions. He's not supposed to offer specific figures about anything but the past. You don't need him for those figures; you can look them up yourself. What you want from him are projections.

> You: Can you give me an idea of what your earnings are going to be like this year and next?
>
> Spokesman: Beyond telling you that we think we're going to have a good year I really couldn't give you any figures. (He's acting correctly here, but watch how we get what we want anyway.)
>
> You: Well, have any brokers or other observers of your company issued any estimates of earnings?
>
> Spokesman: Yes. *Standard & Poor's* has an estimate of $2.25 a share for this year.
>
> You: Do you think that's in the ballpark?
>
> Spokesman: Well, if you don't quote me, yes.

As a general rule, you don't want to ask specific questions. They prompt specific answers, which may be useful but close off the kinds of answers that are often prompted by general questions. You may wind up hearing something that you never would have had the faintest idea of asking about.

> You: Are there any unusual factors in your recent earnings?
>
> Spokesman: Unusual factors? What do you mean?
>
> You: Any unusual contracts or big sales that might not recur?
>
> Spokesman: Well, yes, we did have one big contract that comprised 30 percent of our sales, and that one won't recur.

You: Heavens.

Spokesman: (quickly) But we have a new one coming along that will more than make up for it.

Earnings *can* be deceptive. We like all kinds, but we prefer them to be steady. When profit margins suddenly rise spectacularly, it may be for a special reason. Was that a one-time shot, or will it happen again? We want to be careful not to be pulled into a situation that won't recur.

The first notoriety I received on Wall Street was when I, a fairly green young analyst, got into a slugging match with International Telephone and Telegraph. The company reported earnings in one period that appeared to me to be inflated. I investigated and found out that it had included in its earnings the sale of a British subsidiary. When I pointed this out to investors, a lot of them sold the stock—causing a drop from the high level the stock had risen to on the basis of the inflated earnings statement.

The best safeguard against deceptive earnings is to check sales figures for the last few years. Have they held up? If they've grown along with the earnings, then it's a pretty good bet that you're seeing a stable situation.

But if there's this big, inexplicable bulge in earnings, then it's time to get on the phone and find out why.

The likely answer will be, "Higher sales and higher profit margins." That doesn't really tell you anything. Press on:

What are the chances that the earnings will go down next quarter or next year?

Were these unusual results, something that can't be sustained?

Were there any unusual contracts the company was working on that won't be repeated?

Any unusual products that generated sales for a short period?

Any special accounting practice that may have

produced an earnings windfall—and doesn't represent sustainable earnings?

It's a good idea to write your questions down beforehand, and then to write down the answers as well. If you don't understand what you've been told, talk it over with your accountant.

But the chances are you will understand it because business dealings are really only a larger version of your own family finances. Suppose *you* had an unexpected bulge in earnings? Let's say your company had a fantastic year and paid out a 15 percent Christmas bonus. To what extent can you change your style of living? The answer is, to the extent that you believe your company's progress will continue next year and the year after. You certainly wouldn't go out and buy a house on the strength of that big bonus if you thought you wouldn't be able to make the payments the following year. It's the same with business. There's no point in buying a stock whose earnings have shot up if they're going down 90 percent next year.

Perhaps the most important question you can ask is this one:

You: What are your long-term objectives?

Management should have some kind of a five-year plan. The spokesman may not want to tell you about it but at the very least you should confirm that it exists. I wouldn't let his reticence to talk about it dissuade me, either. Press him as to whether the plan calls for 10 percent growth a year, or 15 percent, or 20 percent. Again, you can get more by indirect questioning.

You: What's the industry rate of growth? Do you know that?

Spokesman: Sure. About 15 percent a year.

You: Well, do you think you can match that?

Spokesman: We certainly expect to do at least as well as the industry. Hopefully we'll do better.

You: I'd rather bet on something more concrete than hopes.

Spokesman (succumbing): Our prospects are more concrete than hopes.

I'll Take It

So now you, an amateur, have done far more than most professionals in determining if a stock is a buy. You've found the company yourself. You've established that there has been little or no interest in its stock by brokers, which may account for its low price. You've established further that its price *is* low in relation to its value, and that the value is there. You know that the earnings aren't due to a one-time fluke, that more good earnings can be expected in the future. You have a feel for that future as well as for the kind of management that's running the company—well focused, confident, friendly.

You really know a lot. If I knew what you know I'd buy the stock myself.

Although you've done far more than most brokers do in investigating a stock, there's one thing you can't do that they can, which is to actually buy the stock.

If I were you, I wouldn't buy through the normal channels. I'd use a discount broker.

The commissions charged by the traditional brokerages pay for a lot of overhead: big offices, high phone bills—many of them run up by salesmen trying to induce sales—and research costs. Discount brokers usually work out of simple surroundings and do no research. Their only business is the buying and selling of securities. They are a relatively recent phenomenon, their existence made possible by a New York Stock Exchange ruling in April 1975, that abolished standard charges on stock market transactions.

Since you've done all your own research, why help pay for someone else's? If you use a discount broker, your savings can be considerable, particularly since the commission rates of some more prestigious houses have actually risen since fixed rates were abolished.

On a transaction of 100 shares of a stock priced at $58, the commission at the bigger houses would be somewhere between $82 and $86; the same transaction by a discount broker would be about $50. On 300 shares at $16 a share, the big houses might charge between $100 and $110, the discount broker, $60. On 500 shares at $18 a share, the big house commissions would run $170 to $183, the discount commission, $83.

Remember, too, that transactions involve a round-trip, unless you hold a stock forever, so the savings when you deal with a discount broker can be twice as great as with a traditional broker. To take one example used by a discount broker, suppose you buy 300 shares at $28 and sell them at $32. Your gross return is $1,200. Your round-trip commissions at the old, fixed New York Stock Exchange rate would be $300.57. Your discount broker's commission would be $150. Your net return, after commission, in the first instance would be $899.43, and in the second, $1,050. Dealing with the discount broker increases your return by 16.7 percent. As the discount broker suggests, you have increased your total return without increasing your risk.

Discount houses offer one other service to independent investors—an opportunity to reduce the spread between the bid and asked prices. Usually, when you buy a stock you must pay the asking price. But the price can be negotiated. The big houses won't bother with that kind of business on small transactions, but the discount brokers will. However, there are two problems in undertaking a small transaction with a discount broker: First, the discount broker may charge you extra for the extra trouble. And you may miss a stock for want of a quarter of a point. After all the work you've done to find your promising investment, it would be a shame to miss it for that amount of money, particularly if you're looking to double your money in from three to five years.

Remembering that the discount brokerage business is a highly competitive one, you might want to check the fees charged by the following firms. Most or all of them will have toll-free numbers. You can obtain these numbers by dialing (800) 555–1212. Or you can write to:

Source Securities Corporation, 70 Pine Street, New York, New York 10005.

Icahn & Company, Incorporated, 25 Broadway, New York, New York 10004.

Quick & Reilly, Incorporated, 120 Wall Street, New York, New York 10005. (This company maintains offices in Boston, Hartford, Philadelphia, Baltimore, Washington, D.C., McLean, Virginia, Atlanta, St. Petersburg, Palm Beach, Fort Lauderdale, and Miami.

Ovest Securities, Incorporated, 7 Hanover Street, New York, New York 10005.

Underhill Associates, Incorporated, 12 Broad Street, Red Bank, New Jersey 07701.

Marquette de Bary, Incorporated, 30 Broad Street, New York, New York 10004.

Brown & Company, 35 Congress Street, Boston, Massachusetts 02109.

W.T. Cabe & Company, 1270 Avenue of the Americas, New York, New York 10020.

Kingsley, Boye & Southwood, Incorporated, 45 Wall Street, New York, New York 10005.

Stock Cross, One Washington Mall, Boston, Massachusetts 02108.

The time to tell others what you've done is after you've bought the stock. Admittedly I'm in a much better position than you are to stimulate the kind of interest that will cause the price of a stock to rise, but you're not exactly helpless. You can apprise your friends of your findings. You can contact an investment club and suggest that its members look into the stock. You can call or write brokers you know, and even some you don't know. You can contact a mutual fund. I assure you they'll be grateful.

If you really think you've found a winner, I'd love to hear from you myself.

CHAPTER 8
When?

It's the most tantalizing question in the game. If you sell a stock and it goes up, you anguish. If you don't sell it and it goes down, you anguish. Is there no way to remove the anguish?

Not entirely. But it can be minimized.

I have some rules to offer you that should limit, even eliminate, your mistakes. But I'll admit up front that I don't always follow them. You'd make me feel a lot better if you followed the rules exclusively, because that way you'd be as certain as one can ever be that you'll succeed in your objectives. But I know the feeling when a stock is moving in the right direction; it's really tough to sell.

First, the rules. They're very simple:

Sell a stock when its price is more than seven times its earnings.

Sell a stock when its price exceeds its book value.

Replace the stock you've sold with another one selling both at the lowest price/earnings multiple you can find and below its book value.

Here's what can happen when you follow the rules.

One day in 1977, I received a call from a broker in Hartford, Connecticut. He told me about a company called Security Connecticut Life Insurance, which was selling at about $9 a share and earning about $2 a share—a price/earnings ratio of under five. The company's book value was

$11 a share, which met the second test. And, to make matters even more exciting, the company was growing at the rate of 25 to 30 percent a year.

On the basis of that profile, I had a talk with the company's president. He confirmed the prospects for growth, as well as the fact that I was the first analyst of insurance stocks to pay the company any attention.

So I bought a block of stock at $9 a share.

In less than a year, the price of the stock rose so dramatically that it passed beyond our pattern. We got out of the stock when it was selling at more than seven times its earnings. In the process, we doubled our money.

Had we remained in the stock we would have made even more money. But we played it safe and by the rules—and then reinvested the money in another stock that was one of the best bargains I have ever seen. The company was called National Western Life. It had a book value of $10 a share, it was earning $1.40 a share, and yet it was selling at only $5.50 a share. Moreover, its earnings were moving up smartly. And so was its stock, soon thereafter. We sold out at $10.

In less than a year the money we had invested in the first stock, Security Connecticut, had quadrupled. *And* we had followed the rules.

The one thing our formula can't do is tell us when a stock will move. We suspect that underpriced stocks, those with the lowest P/E ratios in relation to their values, will tend to move more readily, as well as more significantly. But we can't pinpoint the time. For this reason, it really doesn't make sense for you to think of some stocks as short-term candidates and others as long-term candidates. You should think of them simply as excellent candidates and, once they've performed for you as you had expected them to, sell them.

To Switch or Not to Switch?

Benjamin Graham once suggested that a stock should be sold when you have made a 50 to 100 percent profit. That's a very prudent standard. Even if your stock hasn't gone beyond our boundaries it may be nudging them. You know that when there's been a run-up of 50 to 100 percent in the price, a lot of investors holding that amount of profit will sell. Their sales will put pressure on the stock and its price will drop. Rather than watch your own profits slip away, you might be well advised to sell your stock and buy another whose figures indicate that it's about to pop.

Suppose you've bought a stock that sold at three times its earnings and it's moved up nicely to six times its earnings. At the same time, a stock you've been following has gone down to four times its earnings from eight times its earnings. It might be an excellent idea for you to switch from the one that's gone from three to six to the one that's gone from eight to four. You've made a big profit in the first stock, which may sit there for awhile, whereas the stock that's become very cheap is in a position to make a big move. Sooner or later the stock that's going down runs out of sellers and is likely to jump back up.

If you've got plenty of money to buy the second stock, there's no real need to sell the first one, because it hasn't exceeded our guidelines. But I'm assuming that you have only a certain amount of money; in that case the stock selling at four times its earnings is more attractive by definition because it's at a much lower price/earnings ratio. A stock that moves from four times its earnings to five times its earnings means a profit of 25 percent, whereas a stock that moves from six times its earnings to seven times its earnings will yield a profit of 16 percent.

An even more telling comparison is the percentage change between where a stock is now and the point at which you'd sell it; that tells you what you would stand to gain. Since we hold a stock at seven times its earnings, that means we sell it at eight times its earnings. A stock at four times its earnings that goes to eight times its earnings makes you 100 percent. A stock at six times its earnings that goes to eight times its earnings makes you 33 percent.

If you decide on a program of switching, you ought to have other candidates for your money at the time you sell, particularly stocks that have dropped substantially in price for no reason other than supply and demand.

But if your initial purchase is continuing to rise in price while remaining well within our guidelines, it's another ball-game.

In 1974, I became very fond of a stock called Kemper Insurance. Its price had dropped to $12 a share from much higher levels. I figured it would earn $3 to $4 in 1975, and $11 a share by 1978. Kemper did even better; its earnings in 1978 were close to $12 a share, and its price during that year was as high as $44. Despite this dramatic rise, however, Kemper was *still* selling at four times its earnings, just as it had in 1975.

At this point, a client of mine who had bought a lot of Kemper stock at $12 a share was sitting with an enormous profit. But he didn't sell it, and I agreed with his judgment. The reason was that Kemper, according to our calculations, should be earning $20 a share within the next four years.

If Kemper stock merely maintains the same proportion of price to earnings, it should sell for $80 by 1982. But what if other investors finally get on the bandwagon? Then my client could hold the stock until it was selling at seven times its earnings—in which case the shares he purchased for $12 would be worth $140.

That's not at all unrealistic. *Barron's* has estimated that Kemper's earnings could reach $33 a share within the next 5 to 10 years. So the stock could come close to $140 a share even if it remains at four times its earnings. All this, incidentally, in a stock that is extremely conservative, has a good financial position, and sells way below its book value.

Winging It

So, you see, playing the game very conservatively can make you all the money anyone could reasonably expect to make. But there are moments when it might pay you to elasticize the rules—bearing in mind that when you do you're risking the profits you've already made.

Let's suppose you've gotten to know a company very well. The company spokesman is someone you've come to trust, even though you've never met him, because everything he's told you in your conversations on the phone has come to pass. The company's earnings have continued to be good and, according to the spokesman, there is every prospect that they'll continue to be good and perhaps better than they have been. The company's book value is increasing, too. But the price of its stock has risen to a point where it's equal to book value and exactly at seven times earnings. You're right on the borderline and sitting with a more-than-satisfactory profit. Classically, you should sell the stock. Now, however, you learn from the company spokesman that an analyst for a major brokerage house has written a highly favorable report on the company, and it is to be published momentarily.

If I were in your situation, quite frankly, I don't think I'd sell the stock. Because you can predict with almost complete certainty exactly what is going to happen. The fresh demand stimulated by that analyst's report will cause the price of the stock to rise to a higher earnings multiple and beyond its book value.

Bear in mind that not everyone plays by our rules. To the contrary, we're a small minority. The great majority of investors have never heard of earnings yield and so don't understand the real significance of a stock selling at ten or fifteen or even twenty times its earnings. They play follow the leader; if a stock is rising in price, they'll buy it in the expectation that someone else will buy it from them at a higher price.

Your stock has gotten to where it is selling completely on its own merits. Now it is about to profit from some analyst's discovery. You can bet that his report will stimulate still others, and that these subsequent reports can cause an even further rise in the price.

At this point it's up to you. I can't measure your greed. Nor can I tell you how high a run-up the price of the stock will have because we're now outside the rules. Your basic investment isn't in jeopardy, but you *are* more exposed than you would be had you sold the stock when it passed seven times its earnings and bought something with a low P/E ratio in its stead.

It's all a matter of timing, of gauging the response caused by the sudden exposure of the stock to multitudes of investors. There's also the prospect that one of those analysts' reports won't be favorable, not a likely prospect—because we've seen that analysts operate on the maxim that "negative stories don't sell"—but a prospect nonetheless.

But when it gets to the point where you're telling yourself, "These people are mad to pay this price," then, for Heaven's sake, give them your shares.

Getting Really Rich

There are two theories about how to get really rich in common stocks. The first is to keep replacing stocks with high price/earnings ratios for stocks with low price/earnings ratios. As we saw in the study of New York Stock Exchange securities, this kind of program, diligently executed, produces exceptional results. But the program has its problems. It requires constant surveillance. It involves a lot of roundtrip commissions. And it generates a lot of taxes.

I would almost never make a decision to sell a stock or hold it based on the prospect of paying taxes. The only exception is when it's close to a time period that might make a difference in the tax rate. If you buy a stock on March 1 and the following February 15 it's ahead of your objectives, it probably pays to hold the stock another 15 days in order to take a long-term rather than a short-term gain. But if you've achieved your objective in a stock after holding it for six months, you ought to sell the stock and pay the short-term tax. That client of mine who hasn't lost money on a single investment since he began investing with me never bases his decisions on prospective taxes. If a stock passes beyond our guidelines, he sells it, period.

Switching contantly into low P/E stocks has enabled a lot of investors I know to get rich. But other, equally successful investors believe that a better way to get rich is to hold onto their investments for a long period of time. Invariably, such investments are the kind that they've found ahead of the crowd. These investors may hold an investment until it far exceeds our conservative guidelines, so as to profit from the more speculative temperament of other investors.

Let's say that you pay $3 for a stock that is earning $1 a share. Let's say the earnings double in three years' time, an annual growth rate of 25 percent. Let's say this excellent growth is noticed by investors who believe that you can pay a price for a stock equal to the annual growth rate. It's possible that they would be willing to pay $50 for the stock—twenty-five times the $2 it's earning. In that case, *your* investment has appreciated seventeen times in just three years. That's happened time and time again.

The great imponderable is public discovery. How many investors have discovered the stock? How much are they willing to pay for it? If there is a sudden, significant increase in the volume of trading for the stock on the upside, you can be pretty confident that the price will soar above our guidelines. If the buying persists, so much the better. The moment the buying ebbs, I would sell the stock, or at least lighten up my holdings.

Let me emphasize once more that, playing the game this way, you're risking your profit. Even the most sophisticated investors sometimes lose on this gamble. Benjamin Graham, of all people, is a case in point. He bought Government Employees Insurance Company (GEICO) at 28 cents a share when the stock first went public in the early Thirties. When the stock reached $60 a share Graham didn't sell it, even though it was priced at more than 40 times its earnings. Eventually, GEICO fell as low as $2 a share.

But that's a rare instance. Normally, if you've bought right, you won't lose more than a part of your profit. The worst that will happen is that the price of a stock will drop to a point that puts it back within our guidelines. Against that risk you have the prospect of the kind of play on which fortunes are made.

But your timing must be exquisite. And your information must be fresh. Because selling, like buying, should be based primarily on knowledge.

Following Your Company

It won't take a lot of time and it's not difficult to do, but if you're going to invest your money in shares of a company it's imperative that you track your investment. All that's involved, basically, is following the company's performance.

Prior to the Equity Funding scandal I would not have held out much prospect for getting straight answers from a company about its performance. Companies could, and did, disguise their earnings. If they had a big year they might withhold disclosure of some of the earnings for the following year when prospects might not be so good. The idea was to avoid showing a downturn in earnings that would be viewed negatively by brokers. That kind of hanky-panky still goes on, but not nearly as flagrantly as it did pre-Equity Funding.

You've got to stay on top of your stocks. If you don't, watch out. In the midst of a roaring bull market in 1972 I bought a stock called Centennial Corporation, which had gone public at $45 a share. The stock was selling at more than 30 times its earnings, but that's what I was buying in those days. The advantage of a roaring bull market is that it's very hard to lose. The trend is there, it's easy to find buyers, and everyone is making everyone else look good. Centennial, which never earned more than $2 a share, eventually was selling for $85 a share—and I, to my shame, was telling people to buy it.

Then, because I was suddenly swept up in the Equity Funding scandal, I stopped following Centennial. Before I knew what had happened, the stock was selling for $1.50 a share.

I don't think anyone can accuse me of having illusions about Wall Street. I don't believe that the problems endemic to a business in which information means money have been solved. The biggest problem is still what it has always been, the abuse of insider information. Security analysts run into it all the time. We'll hear that an insurance company has had a bad loss on an oil refinery blowup, but the public won't know of the big claim that's going to affect the company's quarterly earnings. They'll be sitting with their stock when the price goes down, while insiders will have sold out. We'll hear that a company has been approached with an offer for its stock at 50 percent over the market, but the average investor won't hear about this until after he's sold the stock because of its rise in price.

The true insider is the company president who knows his company just got a huge order. He buys stock and the unsuspecting public sells on the way up, not knowing what it has. Or a company official learns that his firm is going into bankruptcy. He dumps his stock, while the public shareholders know nothing about the matter.

There is a solution to the problem—mandatory full disclosure of all information to everyone at the same time, with grievous penalties for failing to do so. The technology exists to make this information available. What's lacking is the will of Congress and the appropriate agencies to make full disclosure the law.

Until that happens, let's not kid ourselves, you're at a disadvantage. But it's nothing like it was five years ago, when, in the wake of the Equity Funding scandal, I urged small investors not to buy common stocks on their own. Today the number of instances in which you might be at a disadvantage has been drastically reduced. You can obtain all the information you need to make an intelligent choice.

I would recommend that you call the company at least each time its quarterly earnings are announced. Furthermore, to be certain that you don't miss the announcement, be sure that your shares are registered in your name when you buy them, rather than in the name of your brokerage house. In that way the material will come directly to you.

Read the quarterly report before you call, and jot down your questions. Again, be general rather than specific. What you're fishing for is the indication of a trend.

> You: I talked to you a few months ago and then bought your stock and I'd like to bring myself up to date. Since I talked to you last have there been any new developments that might affect your long-term performance?
>
> Spokesman: One of our product lines suddenly took off very successfully.
>
> You: Do you think that trend will continue?
>
> Spokesman: Oh, yes.

Suppose the trend hasn't been a good one, that the competition has overtaken your company in an important product line.

> You: How much do you expect that to affect the earnings in the next quarter?

You're going to meet some resistance here, just as you did when you asked about earnings estimates the first time you called. There's a reason. Most companies refuse to estimate earnings, as a matter of policy, because an erroneous estimate can be embarrassing and even troublesome. But they will usually tell you what brokerage firms are estimating. So ask for these estimates, then ask what they think of the estimates. If the estimates aren't what you'd hoped for, you probably ought to sell the stock.

Suppose the stock has been selling at $12 a share and earning $3 a share. That's four times earnings. Now the estimates indicate that the earnings could drop to $1.50 a share. That's eight times earnings—or will be by the time the results are in. You can bet your profit that the stock will sell off when that information becomes known.

The other area of your concern ought to be the company's book value. Remember that this value is calculated by adding up all the company's assets—cash, physical property, accounts receivable, and so forth. Again, ask a general question.

You: Has there been any change in your accounting lately?

Spokesman: For example, have we written down any assets?

You: Right.

Spokesman: Yes, as a matter of fact. We've been carrying a plant on our books at $3 million that we're going to replace with a more modern facility. We've been trying to sell the old plant but we haven't found any buyers.

You: So your book value will be reduced by $3 million?

Spokesman: We'll get something from it eventually.

You: How much?

Spokesman: At least a million.

At this point, you'd want to know exactly what effect that will have on the book value per share of the company's stock. The spokesman may know the answer, but if he doesn't it's an easy matter for you to calculate it yourself. In your copy of *The Financial Weekly*, or some other publication that carries complete tables, locate the item known as "Stockholders' Equity." Reduce it by $2 million. Divide the number of shares of common stock into the new, lower figure. That's the new book value per share. Is it lower than the price of the stock? If so, that might be sufficient reason for selling.

A Downside Checklist

Suppose you buy a stock and its price immediately decreases. What should you do?

First, don't get alarmed. Stock prices always fluctuate on a day-to-day basis; within a certain range this fluctuation is meaningless.

If the stock decreases more than a few percentage points, make sure you're up to date. Did you receive the latest quarterly report? Have there been any recent announcements?

If the stock decreases by 10 percent from your purchase price, then you should definitely call the company and ask questions such as these:

Do you know of any reason why the stock should have fallen 10 percent?

Has there been some change in the company's fortunes?

Do you know where the selling is coming from?

Are any major investors selling?

Very often the reason a stock will go down is that a trust or an estate has to be settled. When any large block of stock comes on the market it automatically depresses the price. But the reason for the sale is benign and the stock should go back up again after the selling has been absorbed.

If you have the money, this kind of circumstance can be turned to enormous advantage.

Several years ago, Carl Mason took a big position in the shares of Meridian Life Insurance. He paid $4 a share, exactly seven times earnings. What intrigued Carl most was that the book value of the stock was considerably more than his purchase price. One day Carl got a call from a broker who told him that he had 16,000 shares to sell. The broker had identified Carl as the only current major purchaser of Meridian's stock. By the time of his call, the absence of buying had lowered the price to $3 a share. "I'd love to buy the stock but I just don't have the money," Carl replied. "I'd have to borrow from a bank to buy the shares." But Carl was tempted. "Look, I'd really like to buy the stock because the book value's so good. I know it's ridiculous but the best I could pay now would be $2 a share."

"I'll call you back," the broker said. A few minutes later he did. "You bought the stock at two."

It was a relatively simple matter for Carl to borrow to buy a stock at $2 a share that was quoted at $3. Meridian never traded below $3 a share after that day. The last time I checked with Carl he still had the 16,000 shares, which were now worth $20 each. His profit: $256,000.

The reason Carl had no hesitation about buying the stock was that he knew the book value was solid. He didn't even have to call the company. He was fortunate that someone had to sell the stock and couldn't find anyone else to buy it.

Most often, a stock that's drifting downward is an expression of general investor unrest with the market as a whole. The drift says nothing at all about the value of your purchase.

But suppose you've bought a stock and its price has gone way down. You'd want to ask the company spokesman if he knows what is causing the drop. He might tell you that he has no idea, that business is fine. More than likely there has been some news item, such as the resignation of the company president, that has caused substantial selling by some major stockholders.

But the spokesman may be telling the truth if he says he doesn't know what has caused the price drop. One of my colleagues, Nick Williams, had been following a stock called Park Ohio Industries for some time with an eye to buying some shares. It had been selling at two-thirds of book value with a price/earning ratio of five, and its earnings were growing steadily. Abruptly, the price of the stock dropped from $20 to $17 a share. He called the company. "What's wrong?" he asked.

"We don't know," a spokesman said. "Things are going great here."

Nick promptly bought 200 shares and urged some friends to buy the stock. In four months, the price rose to $29 a share, a gain of 70 percent.

By keeping in touch with the company, you're in a position to anticipate news. That's the key. If you've already figured out that the news about the company will be good, and the news then comes out as expected, causing an increase in price, you ought to consider selling. It doesn't follow that, because more people now know how well the company is doing, more buying will follow after the initial burst. With that kind of reasoning, you're counting the same news twice, a common error. Count it once, then profit from your diligence.

As to bad news, if you know it's coming and there are no compelling reasons to remain in the stock, you ought to sell it ahead of the crowd. But if you've been caught, *don't* sell the stock when the news breaks, as a general rule, because the market adjusts rapidly after the panic selling subsides and new buyers come in to pick up the bargains. That, of course, raises the price.

There's one danger to mention at this point. Investors tend to "marry" stocks. Either they become attached to a stock that has made them money, or they're unwilling to admit that another stock has cost them money. We don't want this to happen. Getting to know a company on the basis we've suggested might further increase your attachment. Don't let it. If something goes wrong, if the percentages change, then you should sell the stock, no matter how well you've gotten to know the company. There are better opportunities around.

Your Judgment May be Better Than the Market's

What do you do when you buy a promising stock that just sits there for a year or two or three, even though it meets all of our criteria? If the stock still fits our formula, if it's still increasing its earnings and book value but simply hasn't been recognized, it's probably the time to buy more stock rather than sell what you own. Then start talking up the stock to every investor you know.

Let's take an even more upsetting case.

Suppose you've made the kind of investigation we recommend in this book, and you come up with a company that meets the test in every way: a price/earnings ratio of seven to one or less; a book value equal to or greater than the price of the stock. For good measure, the earnings history of the company shows a steady, respectable increase each year for the last five years. Even more, you like what you hear about the company's future, you like the company's product, you like the way you've been treated by management when you've called to ask your questions. It's a picture-book investment in every respect—except that the market goes into a nosedive, and your stock goes down with it. What should you do?

My answer to that would be "buy." You may not want to buy more shares, but don't, for God's sake, sell the ones you have. Assuming the company continues to perform well, you're right and the market's wrong.

By now, you should be able to write the scenario: Suppose the company's stock was selling for $10 a share when you bought it, and was earning $2.50 a share, a P/E ratio of four to one, and an earnings yield of 25 percent. Book value, we'll say, is $12 a share. Now suppose high interest rates and talk of a recession pull the market down and your stock is pulled down with it to $5 a share. The company is still earning $2.50 a share, meaning a 50 percent earnings yield, which is why I want you to buy more shares. The book value is now unbelievably high for a company earning that kind of money—and each year it gets even higher. With the stock at $5 a share, the company would probably pay out 50 cents a share as a dividend. The remaining $2 in earnings would be added to the book value, which thus rises to $14 after the first year, $16 the second year, and so on.

Unless the sky falls in, there is no way that the price of the stock can remain at $5 a share under these circumstances. Either the stock will be discovered by other investors or the company will use the earnings to buy back its shares. In both cases, the price of the stock rises.

If you panic and sell the stock at $5, you've lost $5 a share. But if you hold on and earnings and book value continue to rise you'll eventually come out ahead. At the very least you'll come out even.

Incidentally, the kind of buying you might want to do in such circumstances should not be confused with "averaging." Averaging dictates that you buy a stock and keep buying it no matter what happens. There are no criteria. Our formula tells you to buy more stock—if you have the money—when the price goes down *so long as our principles are intact.*

Now, About That Anguish . . .

It's a lot easier to pick the bottom of any price movement than it is to pick the top, but it's not easy in either case. If numbers were the only factors, it would be a cinch. But buying and selling are more often based on emotion than they are on fact, and almost exclusively so during big market swings, when the action borders on panic. If anything, there is even less rationality on the upside than there is on the downside.

It probably won't do a bit of good for me to say this, but I feel I ought to anyway. Once you've sold a stock there's nothing you can do about it. You shouldn't look back and second guess yourself.

But since you're going to do it anyway, you might as well learn from the experience. Here's a program that might help.

Whenever you buy a stock write down your objective, either in a ledger or on a piece of paper that you then attach to the buy slip. When you sell the stock, write down why you did. Hopefully, it will be because your objectives have been achieved. Three months later, if the stock has advanced since your sale, you'll be able to compare your reasons for selling it to the reasons for its continued rise in price. Only in this way will you be able to alert yourself to the kinds of contingencies that can arise that might affect the price.

But, the market being irrational, the chances are that the stock has gone up for reasons that will later prove not to be sane or sound. You can't kick yourself for making rational judgments that don't work out in a marketplace of emotions.

No one is immune to the anguish that results from selling a stock that is three points higher the day after they have sold it. But here's a question that might clarify the matter: Which will make you feel worse, the loss of the profits you would have made from a stock that went higher after you sold it, or the loss of the profits you've already made? To me, there's only one answer. I want the profits I've already made—and I want them working in my behalf in a new situation after I've sold the first stock. Not only do I have my profits, I have the possibility that subsequent profits in my new investment might match or exceed those I missed by selling my first stock.

That regret you feel when you see your first investment outdistancing the second a few months after you've switched is really misplaced sorrow. The only relevant figure is the comparison when the second stock is sold. Even if the comparison doesn't favor the second stock, that's no reflection on your judgment. You've done the prudent thing; on average, selling stocks in this manner has to come out well.

CHAPTER 9
Insurance Stocks: My Private Gold Mine

There are two principal reasons why many of my clients have made profits of 50 to 200 percent during a period when so many investors were losing money.

The first reason is that they have bought and sold securities according to principles that you now know as well as they do—or even I do.

The second reason is that I have put them primarily into a sector of the economy so neglected by other brokers and investors that I sometimes feel it's a gold mine of my own. I refer, of course, to insurance stocks.

Pause for a moment to consider how much of your annual wage goes to pay insurance premiums. Without even knowing your situation I can assure you that you're in for a shock.

Insurance is probably your third biggest expense, after food and shelter. In some cases, it may be your second. Here are ranges of annual premiums for an American household.

Life insurance	$200	$1,500
Health insurance	$500	$1,600
Home insurance	$250	$1,200
Automobile insurance	$300	$2,000
Total	$1,250	$6,300

If you add in premiums paid for insurance on precious objects—paintings, antiques, rare books, and heirlooms—or for costly items such as contact lenses, the bill gets even higher.

A good portion of your life and health insurance may be paid for by your employer. But *someone* is paying the premium.

An Investor's Dream

From the investor's point of view, the insurance industry is exquisite. It is, in the best sense of the term, the bluest of the chips. It controls more assets than any other industry in the country, more than a trillion dollars. It is all but immune to change. The great social concerns that butt up against other industries make a detour around this one. Insurers do not pollute the environment, nor are they obliged to change their model each year; their customers do not trade in their old policies for new ones every few years, because it would cost them dearly to do so. But what most distinguishes the insurance industry is that, year after year, it makes settlements with cheaper dollars than those it has been paid.

The life insurance industry, which accounts for half of the total product, enjoys a favorable tax position. It functions under its own special tax law. This industry is one of the few that files income tax reports on other than a regular corporate income tax form. It receives special tax deferrals.

As to fire and casualty insurers, the market for their product is all but guaranteed. Home insurance is mandatory; you can't get a bank loan without it. Automobile insurance is mandatory if you're buying an automobile on the installment plan; you can't get credit without it. Even when they pay cash, few motorists would dream of driving without coverage. Health insurance is a must; the cost of medical care is such today that a serious illness to any of its members could wipe a family out.

Insurance is a staple of most families' planning, and a feature of every employment package.

The premiums on all of this business create a tremendous cash flow for the insurance companies. Money not used to pay overhead or settle claims can be invested. So the companies make money twice—first on the insurance policies they sell, second with the mountain of money they accumulate, which is known in the business as the "float." That money is mainly invested in bonds and stocks, creating an investment income that grows inexorably to higher and higher levels. The growth of the average insurance company in recent years has been between 10 and 15 percent in terms of premiums alone. Investment income has been growing even more rapidly as a consequence of rising interest rates.

Insurance companies, in effect, are in the business of making money with your money. They are money machines, creating cash and then lending it. No one in the world lends more money than they do. A rise of a single point in the prevailing interest rate can make them fortunes.

Insurance companies, being for the most part in liquid securities, are far more easily able than companies in other sectors to raise the cash they might need to buy back their own securities—something they might be delighted to do if the price of the stock gets to a point 30, 40, or even 50 percent below its book value. For you, that's just one more protection on the downside; the moment the company begins to buy back its own stock, the price begins to rise.

In most industries, book value can be a matter of interpretation. A company may put a certain value on one of its plants, for example, but how much is the plant really worth? Have competitive changes made it obsolete? Will anybody buy it? And so forth. None of these considerations is of consequence in the insurance business. When you say a company has a book value of $10 million, it's because the dollar value of its stocks, bonds, and mortgages can all be calculated accurately at that precise moment.

In most industries, changing fashions can make today's winner tomorrow's loser. Fashions don't change in the insurance business very much; in fact, they scarcely exist.

Until only a few years ago, insurance companies traditionally paid rather modest dividends—one reason that the public wasn't too interested in their stocks. But this condition is changing rapidly. Dividend increases by the major insurance companies have been quite staggering, in the range of 25 percent a year. Even average-sized insurance companies are increasing their dividends at a rate of 15 to 25 percent a year.

Historically, the industry has had excellent growth as a consequence of plowing back most of its earnings into investment portfolios. And even though dividends are rising, insurance stockholders will continue to benefit from the compounding of investment income.

Year after year, insurance companies roll up some of the most impressive profits recorded. Earnings yields and book values are both enticing. When you add the guaranteed market, the tested companies, the liquidity, the flexibility of price structures, and the invulnerability to fads, you have the dream investment.

So where are the investors?

Your Dream Come True

The insurance industry is exactly what you're looking for—an unappreciated value. Within its ranks are dozens of undervalued companies.

All you have to do to see what a value insurance stocks are

is to look at the P/E ratio columns in your newspaper. You'll see at once that insurance stocks are selling at about the lowest P/E ratios of any industry group. This circumstance has almost nothing to do with the earnings themselves; rather, it's almost totally a consequence of a lack of understanding of and interest in the stocks.

The insurance industry is virtually unknown to the average investor. His basic feeling, without even looking, is that it would be difficult to understand. Even Wall Street professionals feel that way, not for any logical reason but simply because the insurance industry is different from the industrial companies and utilities that they're used to dealing with. Part of the problem is that there is no product that insurance companies produce that you can feel or see or experience. The only rational aspect to the Wall Streeters' reluctance to buy is a feeling that accounting processes in the insurance business tend to be esoteric. The accounting is actually fairly simple if you take the time to understand it, but even few professionals are willing to make the effort.

Fifteen years ago, there were investment firms that specialized in insurance stocks. Today, there are none, unless you count my own. In the entire investment establishment, there are only about 50 full-time insurance company analysts, compared to several hundred in the other major industries.

As an average investor, your chances of finding a company that has either not been found or has been overlooked by Wall Street are probably greater in the insurance industry than in any other market sector. Many of these companies are still being run today by the man who founded them. Such companies usually attempt to raise money fairly early in the game with a public offering of stock. If you can find a small insurance company that is growing rapidly under a vigorous chief executive you can get rich along with him.

Many of the stocks I was recommending in 1977 and 1978 were selling at one-third to one-fifth of the prices that they had sold at five years earlier. Many stocks have fallen from their highs of a few years ago, but few companies have maintained their assets and earnings growth as well as the insurance companies.

In my opinion, insurance stocks have long been the most undervalued group in the market. They are more undervalued today than they have ever been. The Equity Funding scandal is at least partially the cause. Whether coincidence or not, insurance stocks have plunged to unprecedented lows since the disclosure of the fraud. Today, scores of insurance stocks can be bought for from three to five times their earnings.

Think of that for a moment. The most solid, conservative stocks available are also the least expensive!

In 1976, the earnings of fire and casualty insurance companies rose 70 percent. That record is an excellent illustration of how responsive the insurance industry is to inflation. When the industry adjusted its premium rates for 1974 in response to double-digit inflation, the increases proved to be too low, which resulted in underwriting losses of unprecedented proportions in 1975 and 1976. By quickly adjusting, the industry was able to have two outstanding years in 1977 and 1978.

An Embarrassment of Riches

There are more than 400 insurance stocks to choose from—large companies, small companies, rapidly-growing companies, dividend-paying companies, companies selling far below book value, companies selling different types of insurance—life, fire and casualty, and specialty products such as cancer insurance and contact lens insurance.

I don't know of any other industrial sector in which you could apply the test of your own standards as readily as you could in the insurance industry. Is the product useful? Is it one you'd own yourself? Are you morally comfortable with it? It's no coincidence that the company with the most comforting product in the business is also the fastest growing insurance company in the world.

American Family Corporation was started over 20 years ago by John Amos of Columbus, Georgia, It offered a single product—supplemental cancer insurance. The premium for an entire family was $75 a year or less. For the first several years, the company concentrated on the southeastern portion of the country. Ten years ago, it began to expand throughout the United States. Four years ago, it began business in Japan, with spectacular results, even though all Japanese are covered by national health insurance.

Between 1970 and 1977, American Family's total income increased from $18 million to $211.7 million. The company's net worth per share increased 27.6 percent a year in that period, on a compounded basis. At the end of 1977, it had 3.5 million policies in force, and was projecting a fourfold increase in total income by 1987. On the basis of prior growth, that seems more than realistic.

You don't have to be a securities analyst to understand American Family's success. Its product makes sense to the public. One out of four people will develop cancer in his or her lifetime; planning for it financially is impossible. Basic health insurance, vital in any case, doesn't cover the prospect of the calamitous cost caused by cancer. At $75 or less for an entire family, the cost of additional insurance seems more than rational.

Other insurance companies have been slow to realize that the public is attracted to cancer insurance; and even though many of them now offer cancer insurance, none has built a sales force remotely comparable to American Family's.

It's not difficult for an analyst like myself to project the earnings of an insurance company, because a large portion of future revenues derives from policies already sold. Taking into account new business expenses and claims—equally predictable numbers—American Family's growth should be the most substantial of any insurance company during the next five years.

Not for a second should this narrative be construed as a recommendation that you buy shares in American Family Corporation. I have no assurance that something unforeseen won't have happened to the company by the time you read this book. The purpose of this narrative is to show you what can happen when you find a company with an inspired idea just as it is beginning life.

On the basis of today's stock, American Family Corporation traded from below seventy-five cents in 1965 to more then $17 in 1978.

To me, insurance stocks are the glamour issues of this era. The average increase in earnings per share of 25 large insurance companies my research group follows was 68.6 percent in 1977. I don't know of another industrial group with a comparable increase. Because parts of the insurance industry experienced difficult times in the mid-1970s, the price of most insurance company stocks still hasn't appreciated enough to reflect current and future earnings. But those difficult years, brought on by unprecedented inflation and the consequent high cost of settling claims, did produce one desirable effect; they forced many companies to rethink their management practices. The result is a stronger insurance industry, better prepared for future problems.

As of early 1979, it was my intention to make the insurance industry the foundation of my investment program for the next year to two at least. Where else can an investor buy a select, well-managed company in a growth industry, with a book value greater than the price of its stock, huge increases in earnings, selling at an extremely low price/earnings multiple, and with a good and increasing dividend yield that, compounded, could double every three years?

Isn't it ironic that the general public believes the insurance companies to be rolling in money at the same time the investing public ignores them? This makes for one of the truly great opportunities in the history of the stock market.

The Past Is Prologue

You may have noticed that most of the real examples of stock performance that I've used throughout this book have been those of insurance companies. Those performances are history. Today, there are still numerous examples of companies with the same amount of value, the same high earnings yields of 20, 30, and occasionally even 50 percent.

There is a lot to be said against the insurance industry. It is poorly regulated. There is an unhealthy movement of personnel between the companies and the agencies that monitor them; corporate executives become regulators for a spell, then return to corporate life. One of the industry's major products, life insurance, is often sold in misleading ways. The investment policies of many life insurance companies are as antique as their products. But on the whole, the insurance industry performs a necessary public service, a fact evidenced by its size, if nothing else.

The insurance industry has more companies competing on a nationwide basis than any other industry. There are five general types: life, health, fire and casualty, reinsurance, and the large conglomerates in which insurance operations represent the major business. Let's look at each type briefly, from an investment viewpoint:

The life companies

Many of these are among the better growth stocks available. They invariably experience year-to-year growth in earnings, due principally to an expanding economy and its need for more and more insurance. Most life insurance companies enjoy an earnings growth of 10 percent or more a year; the growth, moreover, is highly predictable, because once an insurance policy is sold, revenues from it are derived for many years.

The most attractive stocks in this group are of selected companies 15 to 30 years old, growing at rates of 20 to 40 percent annually in both sales and earnings. This growth is accompanied by a tremendous growth in assets, which in turn creates ever-increasing growth in investment income.

Current high interest rates make matters difficult for many businesses. Not for the life insurers. As the nation's biggest lenders, high interest rates bring them ever greater profits.

Two other factors improve the life insurance outlook still further. Advances in health care and medical science allow the life insurance companies to benefit from greater longevity. And the computerization of business operations creates greater efficiency and profitability.

The health companies

Some of the more spectacular fortunes in health insurance have been made by entrepreneurs providing specialized coverage to specialized markets. Witness American Family. So far, the health insurance companies have managed, with annual rate increases, to maintain their profitability in the face of spiraling medical costs.

While there has been considerable talk about some form of national health insurance, and while such insurance would obviously have an effect on the private sector, I don't see any real risk for some time. First, President Carter's ideas on the subject have not been fully formed. Second, the President seems much more disposed to try to control medical costs rather than construct a mammoth national health insurance program. Third, the overall need to cut government spending in order to curb inflation militates further against such a new program. Furthermore, while some form of federal insurance against catastrophic illness may emerge, private insurance to provide supplemental benefits would still remain desirable to many consumers. People need money when they incur a serious illness and they're willing to insure against it. Remember, Social Security eliminated neither the need nor the desire for life insurance or pension programs.

The fire and casualty insurers

This segment of the industry also experiences steady growth in premium income; it has never grown less than 6 percent in any year since World War II. In recent years its premium growth has averaged 12 percent and its investment income has grown 15 to 20 percent.

Most of the large fire and casualty insurance companies provide all types of insurance, but within the industry some may concentrate on specific markets and products. The largest segment is automobile insurance for individuals.

Many insurance companies specialize in specific coverage for business enterprises. An example is workers' compensation, a type of coverage that has grown at a rate of 12 to 15 percent for many years. Other companies specialize in fire, real, and personal property coverage, still others in liability insurance.

Some of the most successful fire and casualty insurance companies are experts in underwriting unusual risks. They are known as excess and surplus lines underwriters.

Reinsurance companies

These insurers deal only with other insurance companies, and not at all with the general public. Their purpose for being is to spread the risk of loss among various companies in the insurance industry; in effect they insure the insurers against catastrophic loss, primarily by insuring a portion of the insurance companies' risks. Because the reinsurers don't deal with the general public there is little or no regulation of their activities. Also, it takes very few people to operate a reinsurance company; overhead costs, therefore, are low.

Reinsurance is a sophisticated business. Those who have invested in it have done extraordinarily well.

Diversified holding companies

A number of huge conglomerates gain more than half of their earnings from operations of their insurance subsidiaries. Typically, conglomerates are highly leveraged, widely diversified industrial giants; as a consequence, shareholders participate in rapidly appreciating earnings when conditions are favorable. The immense cash flow insurance companies generate is what attracted the conglomerates into the insurance field in the first place; today a rash of conglomerate takeovers of insurance companies has been spurred by the huge increase in the insurance companies' earnings.

In 1977, the Dow Jones Industrial Average was off 17 percent. Insurance stock averages were up 10 to 15 percent. In 1978, insurance stocks also outperformed the Dow.

The key to investing is to purchase value, and as inexpensively as possible. A quality stock that's deeply undervalued is an investor's dream. There are investors' dreams aplenty in the insurance industry—more than in any other sector of the economy.

CHAPTER 10
Tricks and Other Matters

I'm going to assume that you're as human as I am and have a gambling streak in you. Having urged you to invest in the most conservative manner available, I'm now going to show you a method of making money in which you can have a little sport. It's a method that's made me a great deal of money, but I warn you that it doesn't always work. You won't lose very much money in the process; it's just that you may not make any, either.

There is one moment in the year when you can make a lightning profit—anywhere from 10 to 100 percent in a matter of weeks or even days. That moment is at the end of the year.

Although the market is irrational, there are certain patterns you can count on that result from rational acts. One of these is the practice of dumping at the end of the year, stocks in which investors have had a loss. In a sense, even this action is irrational because it's taken without regard to value. But those who do their selling in December have two rational purposes in mind.

The first is to take losses that will offset gains and thereby minimize tax.

The second is to remove bad marks from one's record.

Selling for tax purposes is generally undertaken by individual investors. Selling to get rid of blemishes is done exclusively by managers of mutual funds and institutional accounts. If they don't own a loser any longer it doesn't show up in their year-end portfolio.

Between them, these two selling forces put so much pressure on stocks that have done poorly that they sell off even further—in most cases far, far below their value. That sets us up to take advantage of what I call "year-end specials."

How do we make money in common stocks? By *not* following the crowd. If the crowd is selling, we probably ought to be buying; not always, but often. In the case of year-end specials, we are definitely buyers.

Each December for a number of years I have bought a small group of stocks—different ones each year—that have produced dramatic gains within weeks and sometimes days. The one I remember most vividly was Farah Manufacturing, a producer of slacks. It was the end of 1973; the company had been badly hurt by a strike, and its stock, which had sold as high as $12 a share during the year, had plummeted to $3. I bought a block of the stock—which ran up to nearly $9 a share in a little more than three weeks. In the first three days of trading in 1974 alone, the stock rose $3, so investors who bought on the last day of the year and sold five days later made a profit of 100 percent.

I'm sure you can figure out how something like this could happen. Once those investors with a need to sell the stock had done so, bargain-hunters like myself rushed in to buy the stock. Our demand pushed the price back up immediately to more realistic levels.

There is no other time of the year when sellers are so promptly and surgically replaced by buyers. The end of the year literally cuts the sellers off; once the last day to establish losses or wipe slates clean has passed, their primary reason for selling is gone. They may have no choice in the matter, but you do; their reason for selling becomes yours for buying.

The smart investor who wants to take a loss in order to

THE SHORT, HAPPY RISE OF A YEAR-END SPECIAL

December 31, 1973	Volume	High	Low	Last	Change
Farah Mfg	373	3⅝	3¼	3⅜	−⅛
January 2, 1974					
Farah Mfg	53	4¼	3½	4¼	+⅞
January 3, 1974					
Farah Mfg	144	5¼	4¾	5¼	+1
January 4, 1974					
Farah Mfg	284	7	5⅞	6⅞	+1⅝
January 23, 1974					
Farah Mfg	124	8½	8⅛	8⅜	+¼
January 30, 1974					
Farah Mfg	33	6	5½	5½	−½

minimize his tax would do so at some other time of the year. But few investors do that; either they keep hoping their stock will do better or else they are simply habituated to acting like lemmings.

The best time of all to buy, ideally, is the last day of the year. A lot of brokers and their customers are already starting to celebrate the New Year, toasting their profits or drowning their losses, so you have less competition than you usually would for taking advantage of what may happen. At the last moment, a desperate seller may accept a price he wouldn't accept even the day before. The result? You've got an even better bargain, because you got it at the bid price.

When that kind of selling is going on, you can almost bet that the price of the stock will rise 10 to 15 percent on the first day of trading in the following year.

Finding Year-End Specials

The simplest way to identify potential candidates for year-end turnarounds is to monitor the list of stocks that reach new lows during October, November, and early December. When a stock makes that list, it means that it's selling at a price below anything it's sold at in the prior 12 months. Some stocks will suddenly appear on the list; others will be there day after day, a sign of very heavy pressure.

One very good source for year-end candidates is *The Financial Weekly*, which runs a list of stocks that have experienced the most drastic declines. Yet just because a stock is on the list does not automatically mean that it's a candidate for a year-end turnaround. You have to be extremely careful that you're not buying into a terminal situation, a company with negative earnings and no book value. As we've seen, a stock with good assets behind it rarely sells for less than 15 percent of its book value. Even then you have to make sure that the company's not about to do something like writing off some assets that would reduce the book value.

The one way to avoid getting hurt is to find stocks that meet our criteria. To the extent that they do, you're buying value as well as a quick turnaround candidate, a strong position to be in.

It was toward the end of 1974 that Carl Mason and I became interested in Deseret Pharmaceutical as a year-end special. The stock was selling well below its book value and at a low P/E ratio. Deseret had had one bad earnings period as a consequence of having to recall some faulty products. But we talked to the company and were assured that the trouble had passed. There was every likelihood that earnings would improve dramatically over the next year or two.

Step One on Your Year-End Special Quest

The sample table below, from the *Financial Weekly*, is the one I turn to each fall when I begin my search for year-end specials. Remember: Just because a stock's reached a new low at this time doesn't mean it's a buy. To find the best candidates you've got to do some homework.

New 52-Week Highs and Lows

The following table shows new 52-week highs and lows for common stocks only for the New York and American exchanges and this newspaper's tabulated O–T–C issues, with numbers in parentheses after the name indicating number of consecutive weeks the issue has attained a new high or low.

Summary

	Highs	Lows		Highs	Lows
NYSE	13	65	O–T–C	10	37
ASE	15	21	Combined	38	123

NYSE Highs   (13)

Ansul Co (2)	Bluebird Inc	Mallory, PR (3)	Soo Line RR	Sterndent (4)
Beckman Instr	Fedl Company	New Eng T&T	Standex Intl	UARCO Inc (3)
Bell Canada (2)	Freeport Min (2)	Northgate Exp		

NYSE Lows   (65)

Allied Products (3)	Contl Corp	Hecla Mining	Mesta Machine (4)	Rosario Rsrcs
Am Distr Tel	Contl Group	Homestake Min	Mirro Aluminum	Ryan Homes
Bard C R	Cubro Corp	Ingersoll-Rand	Mo Publ Svc (6)	St Joe Mineral (2)
Buffalo Forge	Current Income (2)	Interlake Inc	Mohawk Rub	Salant Corp
Bunker Hill In	Duquesne Light	IU Internatl	Northn Nat Gas	Santa Fe Ind (2)
Campbell R Lk	Empire Dis El	IU Int A	Occidental Pet	Schaefer F&M
Canal-Randlph	Equifax Inc (2)	Johns Manville (6)	Orange & Ridd	Smith's Trans
Carolina Freight	Fedrid Dep Str (3)	K mart Corp	Overnite Trans	So Pacific (3)
Cascade Gas	Fort Dearborn	Kansas City PL	Pac Am Shrs	Square D Co (3)
Cent Hud G&E	Goodrich B F (2)	Kellogg	Penney JC (2)	Talcott Natl
Chem NY Corp	Grt N Iron Ore	Maytag Co	Pub Svc E&G	UMET Trust (2)
Chessie System (6)	Gulf State Util	McGraw Edisn	Ralston Purina	Uniroyal Inc
Consol Frtways	Hancock Inc (2)	McLean Truck	Realty ReF Tr	Warner-Lambrt

ASE Highs   (15)

Allian Tire Rub	Big V Supmkt	Donnkenny (2)	Risdon Mfg	Southeastn Cap
Ashland Oil Cn	Cdn Super Oil (2)	Hudson's B Oil	San Fran RE (2)	Stanley Aviatn
Autom Bldg	CHB Foods (3)	Iroquois Brands	Sargent Indus	Tejon Ranch (2)

ASE Lows   (21)

Autom Rad Mfg	Howell Indus	Reading Indus (2)	Spector Indus	Winkelman Strs
Branch Indus	Intl Seaway (3)	RET Income Fd	TEC Inc	
Cordon Intl	Natl Paragon	Rockaway Cp	Tri-State Mot (4)	
Giant Yellow	Olla Industries	San Carlos	UDS Inc (3)	
Hall's Motor Tr (5)	Prudential Grp	SGL Indus	Wilson Bros	

O—T—C Highs (10)

Fst Surety Cp	Jenn-Air Cp	Knudsen Corp	Santa Anita Cons	Younker Brothers
Hyatt Intl Corp	Josephson, Marvin (2)	Pacific Resources	Tiffany & Co (2)	Am Bk & Tr Pa (2)

O—T—C Lows (37)

Am Greetings	Grt Amer Cp	Oilgear Co (2)	Tennant Co	Exchange Bncp
Bangor Hydro Elec	Knape & Vogt Mfg	Preston Truck	Tyrone Hydraulics	Fst Bnc Grp On
Bear Creek Cp	NFC Corp	Research Inds	Waldbaum Inc (2)	Hawthorne Fin
Carboline	NatValvMfg	Roadway Express	Webb Resources	Maryland Natl
Champion Products	Noland Co	Rowe Furniture	Wetterau Inc	Globe Life Acc
Chart House	Norell Corp	Scottish Inns Am (2)	Wilson Freight	
Godfrey Co	Nuclear Dynamics	Steak n Shake	Yellow Freight Sys	
Goulds Pump	Oceanic Explor (3)	TIME D C Inc	Bancshares of NJ	

From the *M/G Financial Weekly*. Reprinted by permission of Media General.

Carl and I and a few others bought tens of thousands of shares of Deseret at prices as low as $4.87, more than 60 percent below what Deseret had been selling for earlier that year. Within four months the stock had rebounded to its old high of $13 a share, at which point I sold out. Carl was smarter than I was; he held his shares until 1976, when the company was bought out at $38 a share.

One of the reasons the prices of Deseret had fallen so dramatically, we later learned, was the sale of 100,000 shares in the last few days of the year by Investors Diversified Services, the biggest mutual fund in the country. Presumably, the managers of IDS didn't want to show the stock in their portfolio.

Normally, year-end specials are bought for the short term in the expectation that the response will be sudden and dramatic. But if the value is there, as it was with Deseret, it can result in an even more dramatic long term gain. Carl Mason's investment increased more than sevenfold, whereas mine didn't quite triple.

Normally, year-end specials react quickly, but there are times when absolutely nothing happens for several months. Don't get discouraged when you find yourself in that situation; if your judgment was sound when you bought the stock you should still get a healthy run-up. I bought a stock at the end of 1977 at $2.25 a share. It just sat there for several months, but by October 1978 it was selling at over $12 a share.

I would recommend that you pay particular attention to those stocks on the list of new lows that have suffered the biggest recent drops. Assuming other criteria are in order, you should buy the stocks that have been knocked down the most. Generally this will be at least 40 percent below their highs of that year.

I'd also recommend that you not wait until the last weeks of December to find your year-end specials. In the last few years, increasing numbers of investors have been playing the turnaround game, with the result that stocks often reach their lows early in December, after which buying by the bargain-hunters sends the price back up.

In years when the market is strong you don't get many year-end opportunities. In bad market years, there are plenty of opportunities but that makes it more difficult to identify the stocks with the greatest chance for a turnaround. The best advice I can give you is to pick those stocks that most clearly meet our normal test of value and have also dropped decisively.

"Special Situations"

We used to call them "tips." In recent years, they picked up a more respectable identification. But they're potentially just as dangerous. If someone starts to let you in on a "special situation," cover your ears, sing loudly, and if necessary run away—even if it's the president of the company, himself, informing you of an imminent takeover.

Information *is* the name of the game, and obviously there

are fortunes to be made from advance information about mergers, acquisitions, or other bullish news. But is the information kosher? And will the event it describes transpire?

Unless you're an insider, all so-called special situations— circumstances in which a stock price will rise irrespective of value because of some event such as a takeover—are fraught with risk. It may very well be that Company B plans to tender Company A's stock for twice the current market price, but Company A may decide that it doesn't want to be taken over and Company B may change its mind. Even insiders get caught in that bind. In 1978, I was the intermediary in the prospective takeover of one insurance company by another, in possession of all the facts, opinions, and emotions that are involved in such a matter, and the outcome completely surprised me.

There are other problems with special situations as well. If you get a call from a broker about a special situation, you're probably not the first person he's called. And he probably wasn't the first broker to know about it. The story he's telling you has mostly likely been all over town by the time you hear about it.

Unless you're an insider, a special situation is a speculation, and we simply don't do that. Even insiders often lose money on special situations, which serves them right, because they're not supposed to profit from the information.

Most special situations, moreover, are short-term investments in which you try to profit from the boost given a stock by favorable news. That means your gain is taxed as ordinary income.

Shorting

Don't.

Shorting—selling a stock you don't own at a high price in anticipation of delivering it at a lower price—is, to excuse the pun, a short-sighted way to invest. It's the opposite of what we advocate, that you buy value.

The maximum profit you can make when you short a stock is 100 percent. You'd make that amount only if the company you purchased went down to zero. Why make transactions that can realistically return no more than 50 percent when you can buy others that can appreciate 1,000 percent?

To be successful at shorting, you have to be able to make uncanny judgments about when a stock has topped out. But it's just as difficult to pick the top when you're selling a stock you don't own as it is when you're selling one that you do.

In a period in which stocks are at an all-time low relative to earnings, when more opportunities exist than ever before to double, triple, or quadruple your money, why make a commitment that can possibly cost you a bundle?

Margin

No.

I've waited until now to tell a story about one more man who's at the top of my list of knowing investors. Ed Laufer, as staunch a believer in the principles we've been discussing as I know, joined his first Wall Street firm in 1928. It was an intoxicating time; no one, seemingly, could lose. One man he knew had made several million dollars. The man was buying all the stocks he could, and borrowing money to do so—

meaning that he was on margin and would have to put up more cash in the event of a market break. Laufer begged the man to sell more stock so that he wouldn't be on margin, but the man kept buying stock. He survived the break of 1929, but the next break made him a pauper.

How many horror stories do people have to hear before they'll learn the lesson? The lesson is that you must conserve your capital at all costs. If you lose it you're out of business. No potential profit is worth that kind of risk.

If you borrow money, you're always subject to a call to put the money up. If you haven't got the cash, you're forced to sell the stock at a loss. If you're in deep enough, you lose the stock entirely. I knew one man who had several million dollars invested in just two stocks. One of the stocks was suspended from trading. Because he was on margin he was forced to sell the other stock and he wound up with zero. Eventually the first company came back, but too late for this investor.

If you can make 20 to 30 percent a year on your money, why leverage your investment? By leveraging you might double your money in two years instead of three. For that extra year you risk the loss of your capital.

Buying on margin is like gambling. You can get a big thrill out of winning, but sooner or later you'll lose and perhaps even be wiped out.

Don't do it.

CHAPTER 11
Why the Market's Going Up

Most investors cheer a rising market. They fear a falling market. Before we're finished, I hope to persuade you that this very mentality is what causes so many investors to lose money.

But because the cheer-and-fear syndrome is the prevailing one on Wall Street—the one that powers those giant stock market swings—let me first explain why, in my opinion, we're on the verge of the greatest rise in market history.

And then in the next chapter let me explain why, if you invest in the manner I've recommended, it doesn't make any difference what the market does—why, in fact, your prospects are often better when the market drops.

With the exception of 1974, the stock market as of early December 1978 was at a lower point than at any time since shortly after World War II. Where only a few years ago the Dow Jones industrials were selling at eighteen times earnings, as 1978 drew to a close they were selling at 8½ times earnings. We have to go back to 1948 to find a time in which the industrials were providing an earnings yield of 12 percent. This inversion of price to value is all the more ironic when you realize that the earnings of the companies used in the Index have tripled in that 30-year interval.

Book values offer a second dramatic illustration of how undervalued the market is today. From 1957 through 1968, the ratio of the Dow Jones Industrial Average to the book value of its listings was never below 140—meaning that the stocks that comprise the Index were selling at 40 percent above book. At its peak in 1964, the ratio was at 201, meaning that the Dow Jones industrials were selling at a level twice that of their book value. At the end of of 1978, the ratio was hovering around 88—12 percent *below* book.

To understand why the market is in such a chronically undervalued state, we have to go back to the period following World War II. The country wanted, more than anything, to make up for lost time. Interest rates were maintained at a low enough rate to finance the building of millions of homes and the creation of consumer goods to satisfy pent-up demands. The securities markets reflected both the inexpensive cost of money and the willingness to spend. In those days you could throw a dart at the stock market table and almost assuredly come up with a winner. Glamor stocks were selling at fifty times their earnings, with no one bothering to explain what that really meant.

Before long, however, stocks were overvalued by any standards; they were no longer making those great capital gains, and at their artificially high prices they were paying skimpy returns.

During all this period, interest rates had been slowly rising. When they reached a point where they were actually returning more money than some overpriced, low-yield stocks, investors had second thoughts about the market. Once it became apparent that high interest rates would be around a long while, stock prices began to erode.

In effect, investors were reacting to the excesses of the 1950s and 1960s, when stocks became ridiculously overvalued. They may not know why a stock selling at fifty times its earnings gives them an earnings yield of only 2 percent, but they know when they're not making money.

Higher interest rates produced yet another problem for

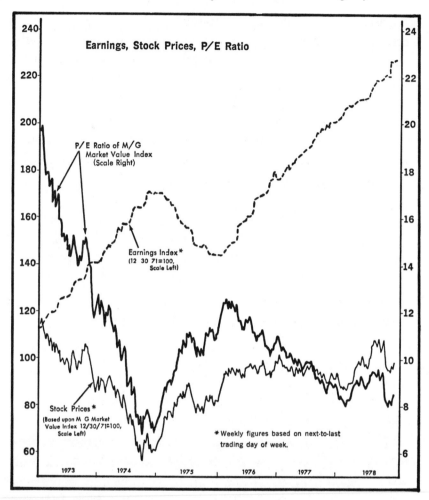

Earnings, Stock Prices, P/E Ratio

P/E Ratio of M/G
Market Value Index
(Scale Right)

Earnings Index*
(12 30 71=100,
Scale Left)

Stock Prices*
(Based upon M G Market
Value Index 12/30/71=100,
Scale Left)

*Weekly figures based on next-to-last
trading day of week.

* Both M/G Market Value Index and Earnings Index are adjusted to compensate for distortions caused by capitalization changes (splits of stock dividends, etc.) as well as for additions and deletions to the list of stocks comprising the index. From the Dec. 4, 1978 issue of the *M/G Financial Weekly* Reprinted by permission of media General.

The Ratio of Earnings to Prices: Off the Charts

The dotted line at the top indicates rising earnings. The lower line indicates the prices of stocks. The ever-widening space between them dramatizes how cheap stocks are today in relation to their earnings.

the stock market and the companies that comprise it. When interest rates were 3 and 4 percent, these companies could satisfy their customers by returning 7 to 10 percent. But with interest rates ranging from 8 to 12 percent, the same companies had to make 15 to 20 percent to justify an investment. You can't make that kind of transition overnight; it requires a period of adjustment. But investors become impatient; they may shift out of their stocks mid-way in the transition. Result? Even further pressure on the market.

All of this repositioning produces side-effects of its own. People get hurt in the process, and their disillusionment burdens the market with the heaviest weight of all. When the burden becomes unsupportable, the market gives way.

The Biggest Panic Since World War II

What really triggered the great selling panic of October–November, 1978? And what did it portend?

To my mind, the panic was attributable to a buying panic that had characterized the market in the preceding months.

Here was the situation. For a number of years preceding 1978, we had seen a two-tier market, one for big stocks and one for small ones. Each group of stocks moved in an entirely different manner. The small stocks, which had been battered in a 1974 selling panic and largely ignored by the institutions ever since, began to move up about two years ago and did extremely well, recovering all the ground they had lost and then some. The big stocks, in the meanwhile, went nowhere. Then, in April 1978, the big stocks finally began to play catch-up. This was a signal for all those investors who swear by the Blue Chips to move back into the market. A buying panic ensued; the market went from 740 to 900 in a relatively short time. All of that feverish buying sent the second- and even third-tier stocks up even higher—higher than their earnings warranted. Everyone was looking for the quick dollar, as indicated by the almost poetic activity of the gambling stocks, which doubled and tripled in a month.

It wasn't irrational that the market moved up; the move was long overdue. What was irrational was the *speed* with which it moved up. The ensuing selling wave was just as irrational.

There is one other possible explanation for the drop. A drop of the same magnitude has occurred every four years since 1954. The last preceding sell-off was in 1974, the one before that 1970, before that 1966, 1962, and 1958. Each of these years is the midpoint in a presidential term, the moment when the incumbent makes his most politically unpalatable decisions. His reasoning? By the time the election rolls around, the public will have forgotten.

Whatever forces created the drop, counterforces have collected that could produce a dramatic rise.

The Arguments for a Rise

In either a buying or a selling panic, the market makes a uniform judgment, irrespective of individual values. With few exceptions, all stocks rise and fall with the tide. But tides invariably reverse themselves, and so does the market.

From a period of enormous optimism, we have descended to a period of enormous mistrust. This fact alone would cause those of us who go against the crowd to believe that a market turn was at hand. Enough believers like ourselves could actually cause the turnaround.

While most investors in the market can be said to follow the leader, it's the small investors who invariably bring up the rear. This is truly unfortunate. They are the ones who most need to benefit from a dramatic rise in prices—to make up their losses, to keep abreast of inflation, and to achieve the kind of capital appreciation that could make a difference in their lives.

I'm convinced that a market movement of this consequence is both inevitable and imminent.

The most compelling reason why the market must rise is the rate of inflation. If inflation holds steady at 7 percent a year, the price of stocks ought to rise at least that much each year, *if only* to reflect a 7 percent increase in sales and earnings due to higher prices alone.

If companies do no better than maintain a growth in sales and earnings equal to inflation, the Dow Jones Industrial Average should double in 10 years even at today's historically low price/earnings ratio. In other words, if investors are willing to place a value of eight times earnings on today's earnings, they ought to be willing to place a value of at least that much on earnings that are twice as great—in which case the Dow, in the 800 range as 1978 was ending, would rise to 1600.

If American companies are able to sustain a growth rate that is even 3 percent above inflation, or 10 percent a year, earnings will double in seven years. In that event, the market, too, should double in seven years, if only to reflect this earnings increase. Actually, a steady growth of that magnitude could provoke the kind of market response that would cause the averages to double far more quickly than earnings.

I can hear you now: "Dirks, this time I've caught you. We've had 7 percent inflation for several years in a row. Why, if prices *fell* in the face of 7 percent inflation, should they suddenly rise as a consequence of the same inflation?"

That's your best question yet. There's no absolute assurance that they will. But I'm betting all *my* money on it. My bet is that the market has finally exhausted itself of selling lemmings. Once the buying begins, the lemmings will once again get in line—at the end of the line—and move the other way.

Why this particular moment for the turnaround? Because the *yields* from investments in stock have become so incredibly tempting.

The Dow Jones Index has gone nowhere in the last 15 years. But the average earnings of the companies that make up the Index have increased substantially in the same period simply as a consequence of inflation. Eventually, stock prices have to catch up to the rate of inflation and at some point move ahead. Companies must make a return on their capital; otherwise there's no point for them to remain in business.

If investor psychology is set aside, the market's future becomes a simple mathematical exercise. The greater the rate of inflation, the more companies have to earn on their capital. They do this by raising prices, and if they can't, they cut costs by making sure that costs rise more slowly than revenues. Those companies that can't achieve these two objectives will go out of business; those that can will not only survive, they'll be very strong.

There are companies that have already made the adjustment to an inflationary society, and they are extraordinary buys. We've learned how to identify their stock—a low price/earnings ratio, a selling price below book value and, in this case, a fairly steady growth rate of at least 15 percent for the last several years. There has never been a greater abundance of such opportunities than there is at this moment. While the market has remained in the same range for several years, the earnings of hundreds of companies have risen dramatically—not just as an expression of inflated dollars but as a measure of increased performance. The result is that many stocks are twice as cheap, relative to earnings, as they were in 1970.

So, while the number of stocks selling at half the Dow Jones multiple is still about what it was in 1970, instead of paying nine or ten times earnings for the cheapest stocks, you can buy them at four or five times earnings—and even at two or three times earnings in exceptional cases.

Each day, more and more stocks come into the under-valued category. Theoretically, if prices don't move up at all over the next five years, most stocks would meet our require-ments for purchase. It's inconceivable to me that that could happen. There would be too many bargains for investors to resist.

There have been occasions during the last 100 years when the Dow Jones industrials sold below ten times their earnings, but never for long. The only decade in which the P/E ratio of the industrials was constantly under ten was the one that included World War II. At eight-and-one-half times earnings, the market has reached a historic rallying point.

History shows that there are periods of overvaluation and undervaluation, but that almost without exception these peaks tend to level out, and prices tend to settle where they belong. At some point, price has to equal value.

The Coming Bull Market: Not Whether, But When?

The cost of money today is higher than it has been in the last 150 years, and perhaps in all of American history. Those corporations that have succeeded in meeting the demand to increase their returns accordingly are excellent investments, capable of returning anywhere from 15 to 40 percent a year.

Never before has there been an opportunity to make these kinds of returns on a systematic, no-guesswork basis. There have been periods when mob psychology pushed prices up at an accelerated rate, but we all know what happens when that occurs. *These* returns are based on the laws of compound interest and solid research analysis founded on the proof of performance of established companies.

In the case of many of the companies that meet our

standards, their stock prices are held down by ignorance or lack of attention. The public's awareness has not caught up with what these stocks actually represent, which makes their market value much lower than the value of the company. That can't last forever. It's like a pre-season sale; you can buy goods for one-half to two-thirds of what they'll cost the moment the sale ends.

Given all these conditions, there is almost no question about the advent of a bull market. The only question is when it will occur.

It is conceivable that it won't. On four occasions—in 1966, 1969, and twice in 1976—the market has reached the 1,000 range, only to fall back. It seems that there is a supply of stocks for sale at that range that keeps the market from breaking through. These stocks are held by investors who had the misfortune to buy at the level and are happy to get even. (They're not even, of course, because the dollars they're getting back are worth far less than those they invested.) But in these earlier market experiences we were dealing with much higher earnings multiples. With prices at historic lows there is a much better chance to break through this psychological barrier.

Once the breakthrough occurs, the market will almost surely fall *back* to 1,000 from whatever level it gets to. That would be a splendid sign. Then the investing public will perceive 1,000 as a *base* rather than a ceiling; future rallies will take off from there rather than stop there.

The one remaining restraint on a rally of 40 to 50 percent from the market's recent position is the high cost of money. Investors who can get 10 percent on their money without risk are highly tempted to do so. But if that competition is removed, if interest rates come down even to 8 percent, investors should move back into stocks in such magnitude that a major rally will occur.

Being on Wall Street every day, I can already feel the

stirrings. Investors like myself have been steady buyers of stocks. Our judgment is buoyed by the presence of so many foreigners in the American stock market.

If many American investors are wary of American investments, the foreigners are not. Why pay fifteen to thirty times earnings for companies in our own countries, they are asking themselves, when you can buy a fine American company for three to five times earnings? Not only have these foreigners been steady buyers of shares, there have been instances when they have moved in and bought up entire companies.

However reluctant American investors may be, the support of foreign investors is one more reason why the value of American companies should rise in the next several years. Investors in Europe, Latin America, the Middle East, and the Far East are traditionally more alert to changes in investing climates, and much more used to moving currencies about than we are; the movement of their capital into the United States market is as clear an indication as we are getting that the market is undervalued.

CHAPTER 12

Why *You* Should Ignore the Market — Whether It's Up or Down

There is one final, critical operation to perform before we send you on your quest: to change the language of the game and the mind-set that goes with it.

If you've ever been an investor, you've undoubtedly thought of yourself as being "in the market." I urge you, now, to rid your mind of that notion.

When you invest according to our formula, you *don't* put your money in the market. You put it into shares of thoughtfully chosen companies. Technically, that's what you've always done, but practically, your decisions have been influenced and even dictated by the performance of the market. Suicide—that's all this strategy is.

The stock market is exactly that—a marketplace in which the emotions and guesses of people interact with facts and figures to move prices up and down. More often than not, the emotions and guesses dominate the facts and figures to the point that they determine the fate of the market. Any kind of uncertainty then sends the market into a nosedive.

If you let that kind of activity dictate your decisions, it can not only cost you your capital, it can lead to an early death.

The very term "investing in the market" epitomizes the problem. It sets the measure by which performance is gauged.

Institutional portfolio managers and professional investors are always trying to beat the market, because they're paid according to whether they do better than or worse than the market. They can lose money and still be congratulated so long as they've lost less money than the market. Mediocrity becomes the standard; if you can beat the standard you've done a good job.

That kind of reckoning may be appropriate for the professionals, but it makes no sense for you. Your view of the stock market ought to be as a device through which you buy and sell securities in publicly-held corporations. Whether you want to own these securities or not is a consideration determined by the *company's* condition, not the market's.

Suppose you were the part-owner of a privately held company. The company had good products, good executives, a good sales staff, and good clients. All the forecasts indicated that its earnings—and your investment—would increase at the rate of 25 percent a year. Would you sell your share in the company? Only if someone could prove to you that your money would do better elsewhere.

Now let's suppose that exactly the same circumstances apply to a company in which you are a part owner by virtue of having bought some of its securities. The company is making money, which means you are too. Would you sell your share in the company under these circumstances? Again, only if you could better your return elsewhere. The stock market may influence the price of the company's stock, but this is only a temporary dislocation if the company continues to make money.

Whether the stock market goes up or down is of no enduring concern to you. It is the fate of your companies, not the fate of the market, that ultimately determines your fortunes.

Some Antidotes for the Jitters

The price of your company's stock on any given day is no test at all of whether you've made a sound investment. The test is what price the stock is selling for when you sell it at the point when it should have fulfilled your expectations.

Ironically, if the company weren't public, you probably wouldn't be concerned about price at all. As part owner of the local dairy or supermarket you wouldn't even know if its price went up or down from one day to the next. All you'd care to know was whether business was good, the company was growing, and expenses were being kept in line.

A lot of investors get very uncomfortable just because they see their stock performing. That's understandable. In their minds, they haven't really bought a piece of a company; they've bought a piece of paper. They're bewildered; they don't know what's happening, because they don't know anything about the company whose shares they bought. They made their purchase because their brokers told them to. The company isn't people and products; it's a name with numbers that go up and down.

When you buy a house you're not buying a deed, you're buying a physical property. It's the same when you buy a stock. You're not buying just a certificate, you're buying assets and liabilities, book value, human performance, and intelligence. It's just as concrete a purchase as though you were going into partnership in a clothing business and bought your share of a building and an inventory.

When you buy a house, you're not buying the housing market either. That market would certainly affect the value of the house if you had to turn right around and sell it. But generally, you buy a house to own it for several years at least. When you finally do sell the house, it is after several periods of ups and downs in the housing market, brought about by changing interest rates or fluctuations in demands. Ideally, you pick your selling time with care, when it's a "seller's market." It doesn't really matter what has happened to prices between the time you bought the house and the time you sell it. What matters is the difference between the two figures.

It is no different when you buy and sell securities. You buy them for their inherent value, not for the play you might get from other investors' fickle impressions.

If you'll invest in this manner—in the same manner in which you invest in a house—you needn't fear the market. To the contrary, you'll learn to understand it as a repository of emotions. You'll learn to manipulate it to your advantage, instead of being manipulated to someone else's advantage.

You must never forget that the investing public consists of a majority of people who don't know what they're doing. They buy on hope, not fact. They sell in fear—either that they will lose the rest of their money or, if they've made a profit, that they'll lose that. Or else they sell because they're induced to by their broker. In any case, they almost never sell on the basis of fact.

This puts you at an incredible advantage provided you're willing to seize it. You must have the courage to go against the crowd. You must act on the principle that the crowd is almost invariably wrong. If the crowd is selling you should be buying. If the crowd is buying you should time your selling to its frenzy and get out at its peak or near it.

A rising market puts a higher value on what you own. So you get rich quicker.

On the other hand, if the market goes up, you have less opportunity to buy bargains.

A higher market tends to produce short-term gains. Long-term gains are harder to come by.

A depressed market provides myriad opportunities for bargains, stocks that are selling miles below their actual worth. These stocks have a much better prospect of remaining within our guidelines for a long period even as they grow in value between 15 and 40 percent a year. They are the classic long-term growth candidates. Moreover, they tend to have strong finishing kicks. We sell them after they have run a long and splendid race, just as they breast the tape.

If you gather from the above that I actually prefer to invest in a depressed market, you're very close to the truth. I believe there is money to be made in any market—*provided*, paradoxically, that you make that one critical adjustment in your thinking.

Naturally, a serious depression in the market can temporarily affect the price of the securities of the companies in which you've invested. But that's the time to raise more money, if you can, to buy more shares of the company—because as we've seen, the return on those shares is even greater than the return on the initial shares bought at a higher price.

Many investors buy stocks in much the same manner as they flip coins. Heads you win, tails you lose. If you flip coins long enough, the best you can expect to do is break even. It's the same with investing in the market. If you follow the charts and the average, you're going to lie awake nights worrying about your investment. But if you remember that your companies will make money regardless of what happens to the stock market, then you'll have peace of mind and the kind of mental perspective that's essential for making a profit.

If your calculations are correct, and if nothing of an extraordinary nature happens to the company in which you've invested, the only way the price of your stock won't go up eventually is if the world comes to an end.

The Doomsayers: They Never Say "Buy"

Prophets of doom like James Dines make a business of being gloomy. It's a very profitable business; you have no idea how many people will pay money to find out what terrible things are going to happen, in the opinion of this doomsayer.

Almost without exception, doomsayers continue to proffer gloom throughout their careers, because that's what they sell. The fact is that they couldn't have been right all this time or we'd all be out of business.

These doomsayers make their biggest splash when the market is at a bottom. They're riding high because they've been able to predict the market that's just occurred. They *never* say, "The market's bottomed out. Now's the time to buy."

Certainly, if the value of the American dollar goes to zero, you're going to lose money on your investments. But you would have lost money if you'd had it in the bank or under your mattress. Actually, you'd be far better off with shares in good companies. They would still be in business, and your stock would still be worth something eventually.

By definition, it is more difficult to make money in bad times. But the good companies will survive them. They all survived the Depression.

When you see a company with a good record in a "bad time" you should recognize that record for the unmistakable sign it is. Don't listen to what the market is saying about the stock; listen to your own voice of reason.

Not everyone survives bad times, but those who do are like the last people in a poker game; they've got all the chips.

Bad times economically can create even worse times in

the market. A company's earnings may drop 20 percent in a recession year, but the market will drop its price 50 percent. The value stays up, the price goes down. Prices fluctuate a lot more than values. If the value is there and the price has dropped, you've found an ideal investment.

When the selling averages of the Dow Jones industrials fall below their book values, you can be pretty confident that you're buying securities at or near the bottom of the market. The Dow Jones industrial average has never remained below book value for an entire year.

The time to be out of common stocks entirely is when there are none available that meet our criteria. With 6,000 stocks to choose from, it's pretty hard to imagine such a time. But there might be times when stocks that qualify might be so difficult to locate that it might not be worth the effort. Fortunately, we're a long way from the point when such a condition would exist. The stock market can only go up so fast. You have plenty of time to gain the experience you need to make use of our guidelines—and make the kind of money that can really improve your life.

If you buy stocks yielding 15 to 40 percent you're going to make money regardless of whether the market goes up or down in the next 5 to 10 years. There's no question that you would make more money in a bull market when optimistic investors will pay higher multiples for stocks. Prices go in tandem; when the Dow Jones stocks rise 20 percent, other stocks will rise with them; some more, others less, but all in the same direction.

What you know that most other investors don't know is that the lowest P/E stocks perform better than other stocks in any kind of market. They may be temporarily depressed, but they invariably rebound. You just have to hold them.

Make sure that the money you're investing is money

WHY BLUE CHIPS ARE GREAT MARKET INDICATORS BUT POOR "HEADS YOU WIN, TAILS YOU WIN" INVESTMENTS

When the P/E ratios of the Blue Chips either fall within our limits or approach their five year average lows, as they had on December 4, 1978 (see chart below), you can be almost positive that the market is at or near its bottom. When the P/E ratios approach their five year average highs, you can be pretty certain that the public has finally gotten back into the market—almost always a sign the market is topping out. Blue Chips are usually good investments only when the market is near its bottom and starting up. If you feel that, unlike the rest of us, you are able to guess the bottom of the market or the beginning of a trend, you might do well in Blue Chips. But why take the chance when there are so many stocks that perform well regardless of the market.

	History				Earnings			P/E Ratio			Dvds	
	52-Week		5-Year		Last 12Mos	% Ch	5-Yr. Growth	Today	5-Year Avg.		Indic. Amt	Yield
	High $	Low $	High $	Low $	$	%	%		High	Low	$	%
Dow Jones Ind.	907.74	742.12	1051.70	577.60	100.51	14.65	1	8.1	12.5	7.3	48.74	6.0
Allied Chemical	45.63	30.00	54.25	23.00	4.60	5.93	5	6.7	11.2	7.0	2.00	6.5
Alcoa	53.00	38.50	61.25	25.88	7.08	31.11	17	6.6	16.7	9.7	2.00	4.3
Am Brands	53.00	39.38	53.00	27.75	6.79	28.60	8	7.4	9.4	7.0	4.00	8.0
Am Can	43.38	34.63	43.38	22.50	5.91	17.96	11	6.0	8.2	6.3	2.70	7.6
Am Tel & Tel	64.63	56.88	65.63	39.63	7.67	14.14	10	8.0	10.3	8.4	4.60	7.5
Bethlehem Stl	27.13	19.13	48.00	18.25	3.88	NE	26	5.2	8.0	5.3	1.00	5.0
Chrysler Cp	13.75	9.25	44.25	7.00	5.14	NE	33	NE	7.9	3.7	.40	4.2

Company												
Dupont Corp	138.38	97.63	203.50	84.50	14.07	33.87	6	8.8	18.6	12.1	7.25	5.9
Eastman Kodak	68.13	41.13	151.75	41.13	4.94	24.75	3	12.4	29.7	17.9	2.50	4.1
Esmark	32.63	23.38	42.00	16.41	3.67	4.92	2	6.5	8.7	5.8	1.84	7.7
Exxon	53.63	43.00	56.88	27.44	5.57	1.59	2	9.0	9.0	6.6	3.40	6.8
Gen Electric	57.63	43.63	75.88	30.00	5.26	13.85	14	9.2	18.0	11.9	2.60	5.4
Gen Foods	35.25	26.50	36.13	16.00	3.94	23.51	12	7.9	10.9	7.5	1.54	5.3
Gen Motors	66.88	54.00	84.63	28.88	11.99	7.73	21	4.6	11.1	6.5	6.00	10.8
Goodyear Tire	18.50	15.38	31.88	11.75	2.73	9.60	4	5.8	11.5	6.9	1.30	8.2
Inco Ltd	19.63	13.38	40.13	13.38	.72	64.71	27	21.0	15.1	8.7	.40	2.6
Intl Harvester	44.88	26.25	44.88	16.75	6.74	15.02	15	5.2	7.2	4.5	2.10	6.0
Intl Paper	49.25	35.13	79.75	31.63	4.58	1.29	3	8.6	13.2	7.9	2.00	5.1
Johns Manville	34.75	22.88	38.25	14.38	5.26	46.52	15	4.4	10.8	6.8	1.80	7.8
Minn Mng Mfg	66.00	43.00	91.63	43.00	4.51	32.65	12	13.5	26.7	18.4	2.00	3.3
Owens-Illinois	24.75	18.00	31.63	13.75	3.04	1.33	6	6.3	9.6	6.6	1.15	6.0
Proct & Gambl	93.00	73.38	120.00	67.00	6.39	10.55	13	13.7	22.2	16.4	3.00	3.4
Sears, Roebuck	30.25	20.00	61.63	20.00	2.62	7.09	9	8.2	22.3	14.1	1.27	5.9
Std Oil Cal	48.88	34.25	48.88	20.13	5.88	1.03	3	7.9	7.6	5.1	2.60	5.6
Texaco	27.75	22.13	43.13	20.00	2.81	20.40	11	8.6	8.5	6.2	2.00	8.2
Union Carbide	43.25	34.50	76.75	29.25	5.79	4.61	0	6.1	9.5	6.1	2.80	7.9
US Steel Corp	32.58	22.13	59.38	17.84	1.83	26.21	23	12.6	12.0	7.3	1.60	7.0
Unit Technols	52.50	32.25	52.50	10.38	4.54	14.29	17	8.3	9.6	5.7	2.00	5.2
Westinghouse	25.00	16.25	47.38	8.00	3.46	18.49	15	5.1	12.9	6.4	.97	5.5
Woolworth FW	23.00	17.13	31.88	8.00	3.81	49.41	7	5.1	9.0	4.9	1.40	7.2

From the Dec. 4, 1978 issue of the *M/G Financial Weekly.* Reprinted by permission of Media General.

you're not going to need in the short term. If you buy a stock at five times its earnings, and it drops to four times its earnings and you have to have your money, that's a loss of 20 percent. You've got to use money you're not suddenly going to have to pull out of the market at a bad time, money that won't radically alter your life, if you lose it.

I can't tell you, or even ask you, to take a risk. I can only point out the consequences if you don't.

I know where my money's going to be invested—100 percent in common stocks. I'm not typical. I'm a bachelor. I have no home on which I make mortgage payments. I don't even have an insurance policy. My parents are dead. No one's life will be affected in the slightest if I go broke or even when I die. The only people I support are my attorneys.

But I like to live well and enjoy life and help others who haven't been as fortunate as I have been. Being human, I like to make the most of what I have. I certainly don't want to see my money wither away as a consequence of inflation. In these respects, I'm sure I'm very much like you.

Forget about the market. Just maintain your investment in companies whose products you like, whose managements you like, whose business logic seems sound, and whose results, measured in a precise, arithmetic way, are giving you a return you like.

If you'll just play the game this way, you'll be a investor. You won't lose your money—and you won't lose any sleep.

The economic rewards in our society go to those who have built successful companies. You can participate in that; you can take advantage of the system; you can make a fortune. Getting into a company that's selling below its value is better than getting in on the ground floor; you're getting on in the basement just as the elevator's starting to go up.

APPENDIX
How To Read An Annual Report

An annual report is an advertisement. It makes representations in behalf of the company that puts it out. It broadcasts a confidence in the company's future that may or may not be warranted by the facts. It attempts to put the best possible face on adversity. The basic objective of the report is to inspire confidence in management on the part of stockholders and clients.

You don't *have* to know how to read an annual report in order to invest successfully, as long as you follow the procedures we've discussed in this book. In fact, reading a report can unconsciously work against you; you get the feeling that there's a great deal to know and become discouraged. An annual report tells you much more than you need to know. On the other hand, it does have a lot of interesting and helpful information.

What follows is a glossary of terms and contents that you'll find in almost every annual report, with an analysis of what they mean.

Financial Highlights

Most annual reports will have a section called Financial Highlights in which key figures are given. These are some of the things you can expect to see.

177

Net Sales

These are total revenues for the fiscal year. A two-year comparison is given, and is usually accompanied by percentage change year to year. You should adjust it for inflation to see a company's real growth.

Earnings Before Income Taxes

This is the net earnings of the company before they pay their taxes. Percentage change shows improvement or deterioration in margins when compared to percentage change in sales.

Net Earnings

These are the company's earnings after they pay their taxes. These are their actual earnings, but the pretax earnings change is more significant as far as the actual condition of the company is concerned.

Dividends Paid

This is the total amount of dividends paid by the company during the year. It is also an indication of the board of directors' perception of the future of the company. Dividends are usually increased when a company feels that things will continue to improve in the future. Recently, this indication has come under increasing debate as more and more directors have raised dividends to keep stockholders happy, rather than as an indication of future performance.

Capital Expenditures

Capital Expenditures are investments to increase capacity or bring on new products. In periods of accelerating expansion this should grow year to year at amounts greater than inflation—

characteristic of growth companies. Capital Expenditures should also be greater than Depreciation and Amortization to show net growth in Property, Plant and Equipment.

Depreciation and Amortization

All assets are depreciated over their expected lifetime. The figure given here is the total amount by which the company's assets have been depreciated. It is advantageous to quickly depreciate assets since this is a deduction from income taxes. (By dividing the property, plant and equipment by the depreciation and amortization for one year, one can obtain the average lifetime of the assets.)

Year-End—

Working Capital

This is a good indication of the financial conditions of the company. It is the amount of money that the company has available to work with during the year. It is found by subtracting Current Liabilities from Current Assets. The definitions of Current Assets and Current Liabilities are, respectively, those assets which can be liquidated and those debts that will come due within a year. (See Balance Sheet.)

Property, Plant and Equipment (Net)

This figure is the net amount of these assets usefully employed by the company. The actual cost is much higher but the accumulated depreciation on these assets has been deducted from the total cost. If one asset suddenly becomes obsolete, it will be written off.

Stockholder's Equity

This is the book value of the company. Usually, the per share figure is included, but if not, it can be obtained by dividing the figure given by the number of shares outstanding.

Per Share

Net Earnings

Same as above, except the figure was divided by Average Shares Outstanding to get the per share figure.

Dividend Paid

Per Share dividends declared and paid by the company during the year.

Average Shares Outstanding

When shares outstanding change during the year, the average number outstanding is calculated on a time-weighted basis. This is deemed a more relevant measure than using year-end shares outstanding.

Statistics

Net Earnings as a Percent of Net Sales

Self-explanatory, also known as the Net Margin. In some cases you can discover significant deterioration of improvement in the margin. It can be the result of changes in productivity, varying expenses, technological advances, or something unrelated to the basic profitability, such as a change in the company's tax burden.

Return on Average Stockholder's Equity

Net earnings divided by Stockholder's Equity. An indication of how well the company is employing its book value. It is often interesting to compare return on average stockholders' equity to prevailing inflation, interest rates, and earnings yield on the stock.

Ratio of Current Assets to Current Liabilities

Known as the Current Ratio. This is an indication of the short-term financial strength of a company. If it is too low, the company may have trouble meeting its short-term debts and could find itself in a financial predicament. If it is too high, a closer inspection is warranted since the company may not be employing its assets efficiently. Also, certain of the company's current assets may be dangerously high. High inventories are indicative of sales not meeting expectations, or perhaps of the failure of a certain product (e.g., citizens band radio market collapse). High Accounts Receivable might indicate the possible default of a customer (e.g., a customer might owe $100,000, if he is about to go bankrupt, but the $100,000 might still appear in Accounts Receivable although there is very little chance of collecting). These two items should keep pace with the growth in sales. If there is a significant disparity, it should be examined, Accounts Receivable are generally due in a month or so. If Accounts Receivable grow steadily in relation to sales, it probably means that some of the accounts are getting quite old and, as they get older, the chances of having them be paid declines.

Ratio of Stockholder's Equity to Long-Term Debt

This is a measure of the conservatism of the company's management. A very conservative company has almost no debt; thus, this ratio will approach infinity. An aggressive company would have a very low ratio since it would try to borrow as much money as possible. A couple of points should be mentioned: 1) When interest rates go up, companies with a low ratio have profit squeezes as their debt expenses soar; but when interest rates are low and money is cheap, their profitability could be greatly enhanced. 2) Average ratios will vary from industry to industry, so the ratio should be compared to the industry average and not to an absolute number (e.g., the utility industry is highly leveraged [low ratio], while the insurance industry has almost no debt).

Net Sales

These are the total revenues for the fiscal year.

Cost of Goods Sold

This is the cost to the company of materials and production of the products they sell.

Gross Profit

Gross Profit is the difference between Net Sales and Cost of Goods Sold.

Operating Expenses

Operating Expenses are the expenses attributable to the operation of company. They will usually be broken down and are subtracted from the gross profit. Be on the lookout for significant changes.

Administrative Expenses

Generally the expenses of the home office (executives). A good sign would be a constant figure here as sales increased since this would indicate an increase in white collar productivity.

Product Research and Engineering
This is the development cost for new products and it is a good indication of work being done that will affect the future performance of the company. Except for something like Kleenex, technological progress must constantly be made for a company to stay abreast of the market.

Earnings from Operations
Income after deducting Operating and Development Expenses from Gross Profit.

Other Income and Expense
These are items not related to operations. The following are examples of some you might encounter.

Interest Expense
Cost of financing debt.

Other Income
Miscellaneous and usually insignificant, but it could be significant in such cases as gains on sales of assets.

Income Taxes
We all pay them at some time. There are deductions or changes in tax rates explained in the footnotes.

Net Earnings
This is the income of the company after it has paid its taxes.

Earnings Per Common Share
Net Earnings divided by Average Shares.

Balance Sheet

The basic equation of a balance sheet is the following:

Total Assets = Total Liabilities + Stockholders' Equity

Assets are found on the left side of the balance sheet while Liabilities and Stockholders Equity are on the right side. In this section I shall highlight the balance sheet items of particular interest.

Assets

Current Assets

Current Assets are those assets that can be liquidated within a year.

Accounts Receivable

Sales that have been made but have not yet been paid for. This is the money due the company from its customers. Sales are usually made under conditions allowing the customer 30 to 60 days to pay the bill. In a financially healthy company receivables should remain at a constant (or declining) percentage of sales. It is quite likely that some of a company's accounts receivable are becoming doubtful if the accounts receivable are rising as a percentage of sales.

Inventories

Inventories are maintained to fill sales. They are especially important for standardized, non-custom products. They should be maintained at proper levels to allow prompt delivery. Maintaining too high a level would be very expensive and maintaining too low a level could cause the company to lose customers and orders owing to late deliveries and unavailable goods. Inventories should thus stay in step with sales. In periods of growth they should expand, and in periods where economic growth looks unlikely, the company should be contracting its inventories.

Property Plant & Equipment

Land, Buildings and Machinery
These make up the productive capital assets of the company. You should try to find out if they are obsolete or technologically well advanced.

Accumulated Depreciation
This is the total amount that the specific assets listed in the Land Building and Machinery categories have been depreciated over their entire lifetimes. (For instance, when an asset is sold its accumulated depreciation is deducted from this total). From examining this figure one can determine the philosophy of management on depreciation. But one can also get an idea of the age of the assets employed. If they had been 80 percent depreciated, it would be indicative of ancient machinery which is probably almost worn out and most likely inefficient and very expensive to replace. This is generally pretty important for our analysis of undervalued companies in which this may sometimes be the case.

Other Assets

Patents, Trademarks and Other Sundry Assets
These are usually deducted from stockholders' equity, as they are not easily sold and are generally balance sheet padding or appear just for the record. Most companies will write these off over a number of years.

Liabilities and Stockholders' Equity

Current Liabilities
Current Liabilities are those liabilities that will come due within one year including the maturation of long-term debt, bank loans, accounts payable, and so forth. As long as there is enough to more than cover these liabilities in the Current Assets section, there shouldn't be any trouble. You just have to watch out for extraordinary items, such as a bubble in any particular item.

Long-Term Debt
These are obligations of greater than one year in maturity, including bonds, senior notes, and long-term leases. Long-term debt is significant in that it represents the amount of leverage employed by the company. It is critical in periods of changing interest rates. The amount of long term debt also provides an indication of the fixed interest charges a company has. This can be devastating for a company with declining sales.

Stockholders' Equity

This is the book value; it is generally made up of three sections.

Common Stock

The shares authorized to be sold and those that have been issued are listed here. Par Value is an accounting figure used to give an indication in the balance sheet of the number of shares outstanding. The actual Par Value per share is meaningless.

Additional Contributed Capital

Is the amount in excess of Par Value that the company sold its shares for. When the figure is low it means that except for small sales to employees, no significant sales of stock have been made since the company's inception. It shows that the company has been able to fund its growth internally. In many companies, this figure is far greater than the Par Value figure, especially if these companies have an unabated hunger for equity capital. This is quite commonly seen in utility companies.

Retained Earnings

These are the accumulated earnings of the company that have not been paid out to the stockholders. This is usually the major category in the Stockholders' Equity Section. When the company has a loss, it is deducted from this category. So it also serves as padding for the company. A company earning $2 a share but with deficit retained earnings does not have any margin of safety with which to protect itself from losses without risking its financial solvency.

Auditors' Report

Usually this is a simple statement to the effect that they have examined the financial statements and that they meet generally accepted accounting criteria. These should always be read because there could be any number of qualifications that could be potentially material.

The Notes to the Financial Statements

These are an integral part of Financial Statements, but since they vary from company to company they are not worth explaining in detail. Instead, a plea to the reader to examine them carefully is much more important. These Notes generally contain quite a bit of information that is critical for the analysis of Financial Statements. They will explain such things as the sales of assets and the write-down of inventories.

Management's Analysis of Financial Results

Generally this provides good reading and does not need an explanation. It will get the up and coming analyst off to a start sorting out the figures.

Historical Figures

Usually these are only given for five years, but they will give an idea of the consistency of management, the growth in earnings and sales, past problems, and trends. It should be studied carefully.

Stock Price history is usually given. One should try not to buy near historic highs. One can also get an idea of volatility; if a stock sells at the same price through good and bad times, it probably isn't going to be a great performer unless there is a big change. Benjamin Graham, for example, did not like to buy unless a stock had dropped forty percent below its high.

You can usually find the name of the shareholder contact at the company inside the back cover of the annual report.

The Form 10-K

To the average investor, the 10-K is usually a big disappointment when first received. It is not a beautiful glossy production like the annual report. But, while it contains the same financial statements as the annual report, it must also answer questions specified by the SEC. All public companies must file these with the government and make them available to the shareholders (although not always free of charge).

The Form 10-K will include such things as descriptions of a company's business, divisions, competition, employees, and customers as well as discussions of the various parts of the financial statements.